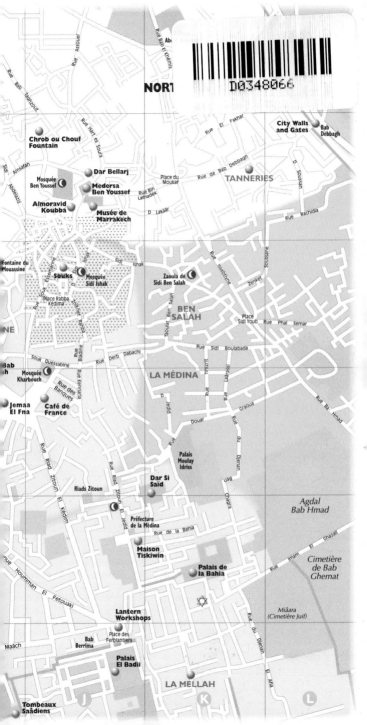

NORT

D0348066

Chrob ou Chouf Fountain

Rue Bab Taghzout
Rue Assouel
Rue El Khemis
Rue Ab
Rue Hart es Soura

City Walls and Gates

Bab Debbagh

Rue El Fakhar

Dar Bellarj

Place du Mouker

Rue de Bab Debbagh

TANNERIES

Mosquée Ben Youssef

Medersa Ben Youssef

Rue Bin Lafnadek

Sidi Amsafah
Sidi Abdelaziz

D La.aâr

Almoravid Koubba

Musée de Marrakech

Rue Rachidia

D Soussan

Fontaine du Mouassine

Souks

Rue Essaffrine

Sidi Ishak

Mosquée Sidi Ishak

Zaouia de Sidi Ben Salah

Rue Issebchyne

Zenket

Place Rabba Kédima

Rue Zinkel

Rahba

BEN SALAH

Place Sidi Youb

Rue Phal Semar

NE

Souk Ouessabine

Rue Kennaria

Rue Derb Dabachi

Rue Sidi Boulabada

LA MÉDINA

Taoudir Ben Salah

Rue Issebchyne

Bab sh

Mosquée Kharbouch

Rue des Banques

D Jedid

Rue Tihzirt

Rue Ladrassi

Rue Graoua

Rue Ba Hmad

Jemaa El Fna

Café de France

Douar

Rue du Dienan

Rue Riad Zitoun El Kédim

Palais Moulay Idriss

Riads Zitoun

Dar Si Said

Agdal Bab Hmad

Rue Riad Zitoun El Jedid

Préfecture de la Médina

Rue de la Bahia

Rue Imam El Ghazali

Cimetière de Bab Ghemat

Avenue Houmman El Fetouaki

Maison Tiskiwin

Palais de la Bahia

Rue du Dienan

Maâch

Lantern Workshops

Place des Ferblantiers

Miâara (Cimetière Juif)

Bab Berrima

Palais El Badii

Rue du Dienan

El Afia

LA MELLAH

Tombeaux Saâdiens

J

K

L

CITYPACK TOP 25
Marrakech

JANE EGGINTON

If you have any comments
or suggestions for this guide
you can contact the editor at
Citypack@theAA.com

AA Publishing
Find out more about AA Publishing and the wide
range of services the AA provides by visiting our
website at www.theAA.com/travel

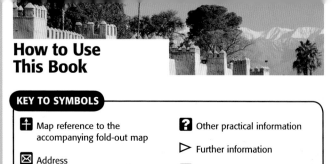

How to Use This Book

KEY TO SYMBOLS

✚ Map reference to the accompanying fold-out map

✉ Address

☎ Telephone number

🕐 Opening/closing times

🍴 Restaurant or café

🚆 Nearest rail station

Ⓜ Nearest subway (Metro) station

🚌 Nearest bus route

⛴ Nearest riverboat or ferry stop

♿ Facilities for visitors with disabilities

❓ Other practical information

▷ Further information

ℹ Tourist information

✋ Admission charges: Expensive (over €9), Moderate (€3–€9), and Inexpensive (€2 or less)

★ Major Sight   ★ Minor Sight

👣 Walks   🚐 Excursions

🛍 Shops

🎭 Entertainment and Nightlife

🍴 Restaurants

This guide is divided into four sections
• Essential Marrakech: An introduction to the city and tips on making the most of your stay.
• Marrakech by Area: We've broken the city into five areas, and recommended the best sights, shops, entertainment venues, nightlife and restaurants in each one. Suggested walks help you to explore on foot.
• Where to Stay: The best hotels, whether you're looking for luxury, budget or something in between.
• Need to Know: The info you need to make your trip run smoothly, including getting about by public transport, weather tips, emergency phone numbers and useful websites.

Navigation In the Marrakech by Area chapter, we've given each area its own colour, which is also used on the locator maps throughout the book and the map on the inside front cover.

Maps The fold-out map accompanying this book is a comprehensive street plan of Marrakech. The grid on this fold-out map is the same as the grid on the locator maps within the book. We've given grid references within the book for each sight and listing.

Contents

Introducing Marrakech

Marrakech may only be a short flight from Europe, but it is undeniably exotic. An ancient desert trading post and once the cultural centre of the Islamic world, it is now one of the world's most desirable travel destinations.

This is a city to stimulate the senses. Marvel at the serene Islamic and Andalusian architecture of magnificent palaces and tranquil gardens. Gaze at the art in local galleries, live it up in colonial cafés and decadent hotels, and sweat in traditional steam baths and luxury spas. Be hypnotized by ancient storytellers and snake charmers in the main square against a backdrop of the call to prayer that resounds throughout the day and a soundtrack of traditional *gnawa* music.

The Pink City is named for the hue of its ancient, fortress-like walls that cradle the medina—the medieval centre that both disorientates and captivates. Find your way through the dizzying alleyways of the souk markets to the outdoor theatre that is the main square.

The chaotic and exotic medina is a world away from the extravagant tourist developments of the New City that are straight out of the 21st century. This is Marrakech at its most modern, site of the largest nightclub in Africa and extraordinary resort hotels. Of course there is traditional entertainment too: dinner accompanied by belly dancers, mint tea served by shopkeepers in the souks, and perhaps the greatest, sinking into the pool of your stylish hotel after a day on the dusty streets of the medina.

Within a day's reach of the city are camel rides and sand dune treks through the vast expanse of the desert, and hiking in the snowy Atlas Mountains, dotted with Berber villages. A couple of hours west, you can enjoy the cool breeze of the Atlantic Ocean in the laid-back resort of Essaouira.

Facts + Figures

- 'Vision 2010' is the young king's ambitious plan to bring 10 million visitors annually to Morocco.
- 13 casinos, over 100 international hotels and several new golf courses are currently being built.
- Unemployment in Marrakech is around 10 per cent.

PEOPLE

The people of Marrakech, as in all trading posts, are a cosmopolitan mixture. Arabs joined the Berbers (the first inhabitants, who came from the mountains) and later came the French. They are all generally warm and welcoming people.

- The average wage in Morocco is 110 dirhams (€10 approx) a day.
- Call to prayer occurs five times a day.
- Half the population is under 20.

LOCAL LUXURY

Don't miss the chance to stay in a riad (courtyard hotel). These historic houses provide sanctuary and even sanity in the mayhem of the medina. Invariably infused with the personality of their (frequently European) owners, many offer exquisite experiences, with helpful, personal service that may well be the highlight of any trip.

THE FUTURE

Thanks to a law that says no building shall stand higher than the Koutoubia Mosque, Marrakech is expanding outwards instead of upwards—a property explosion that is peopling the harsh scrubland beyond the city. It is funded by massive foreign investment—an irony that does not escape the Moroccan people who have barely shaken off French colonialism.

A Short Stay in Marrakech

DAY 1

Morning Begin your day with a fresh orange juice from one of the stands on the main square of **Jemaa El Fna** (▷ 24–25), or indulge in a little people-watching at **Café de France** (▷ 32).

Mid-morning Take a short stroll to the omnipresent **Koutoubia Mosque** (▷ 26–27), circling behind it for a little promenade in its gardens and rest a while on one of its benches. For a full circuit, consider a walk around the heart of the Marrakech (▷ 35).

Lunch Have a simple lunch of salad or pizza with a cooling ice tea or orange sorbet on the breezy rooftop of Les Terrasses de l'Alhambra (▷ 39).

Afternoon Dive into the depths of the souks to the north of Jemaa El Fna for some serious shopping and some hard bartering (▷ 36). Be prepared to get lost: it's all part of the experience.

Mid-afternoon Take a well-earned break in the Café des Épices (▷ 76), a charming little café in a square filled with spice sellers on the edge of the **Souks** (▷ 30–31). Sip a mint tea from one of the upper levels taking in the changing art on the walls and watch the scene below.

Dinner Return to Jemaa El Fna for an alfresco feast at the **Night Market** (▷ 28–29). Eat spicy sausages surrounded by storytellers and exotic snake charmers.

Evening Take a romantic *calèche* (horse-drawn) tour (▷ 32) around the **city walls and gates** (▷ 65). When night falls, the traffic dies down and the full beauty of the soaring red medieval walls can be appreciated.

DAY 2

Morning Set off early after a rooftop breakfast in your hotel or riad. Avoid the crowds by visiting the magnificent **Palais El Badii** (▷ 50–51) when it opens at 8.30am.

Mid-morning Watch the tin workers at work while sipping on a reviving mint tea or strong coffee in the little café on Place de Ferblantiers. Perhaps buy a lantern as a souvenir before heading to **Jardin Majorelle** (▷ 82–83), taking either a taxi or *calèche*,

Lunch Enjoy a light lunch with a delicious fresh juice at the café in Jardin Majorelle, surrounded by exotic plants and birdsong.

Afternoon Completely unwind with a hammam (traditional steam bath) and a massage (booked in advance). If your riad hasn't got one, consider the sublime Bains de Marrakech (▷ 58)—although here you will need to reserve several weeks in advance.

Mid-afternoon Dive into your riad plunge pool (most are too small for a swim) and enjoy the tranquillity of a home from home away from the madness and dust of the medina. Enjoy Moroccan tea and pastries on the rooftop before getting ready for the evening.

Dinner Have dinner at Le Comptoir Darna, (reservations are essential ▷ 92), for a taste of haute cuisine, with traditional belly dancing for entertainment.

Evening Pop upstairs to the Comptoir bar, and travel back to the *belle époque* era to join the beautiful people sipping cocktails under extravagant chandeliers.

Top 25

TOP 25

▶ ▶ ▶

Almoravid Koubba ▷ 64
The only piece of architecture from the founding Almoravid dynasty.

City Walls and Gates ▷ 65 Dramatic, ancient ramparts that cradle the old city.

Dar Si Saïd ▷ 44
Attractive 19th-century palace housing the Museum of Muslim Arts.

Tombeaux Saâdiens ▷ 52–53 Burial place of royalty and children from the Saadian Dynasty.

Tiz-n-Tichka ▷ 104
Follow this mountain pass to lively village markets, kasbahs, a mighty fortress and the Sahara.

Tizi-n-Test ▷ 102–103
Enjoy dramatic mountains and mule trekking in the woods.

Tanneries ▷ 70–71 See the ancient craft of tanning in action—a trade passed down the centuries.

Souks ▷ 30–31
Get lost in the maze of these markets. Everyone should wander here.

Palais de la Bahia ▷ 49 The 'Brilliant' royal residence with its superb interior once also served as a harem.

Palais El Badii ▷ 50–51
This 'incomparable palace' contains a medieval masterpiece.

Ourika Valley ▷ 100–101 Pretty region in the mountain foothills, dotted with Berber villages.

Night Market ▷ 28–29
Tuck into an alfresco feast to remember. Plenty of fresh food to choose from.

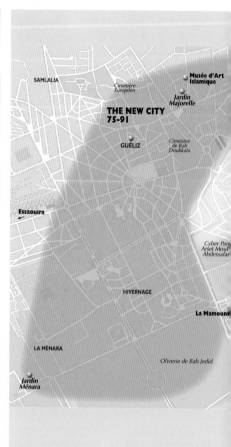

SAMLALIA

Cimetière Européen

THE NEW CITY 75–91

Musée d'Art Islamique

Jardin Majorelle

GUÉLIZ

Cimetière de Bab Doukkala

Essaouira

Cyber Parc Arset Moul Abdessalar

HIVERNAGE

La Mamoun

LA MÉNARA

Oliverie de Bab Jedid

Jardin Ménara

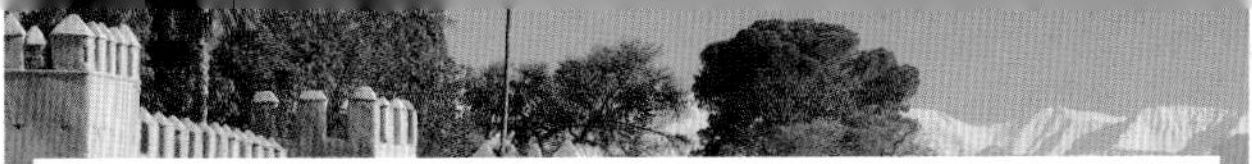

These pages are a quick guide to the Top 25, which are described in more detail later. Here they are listed alphabetically, and the tinted background shows which area they are in.

Essaouira ▷ 98–99 Laid-back seaside resort only a few hours from the city.

Guéliz ▷ 80–81 New City neighbourhood with lovely boutiques and cafés.

Jardin Majorelle ▷ 82–83 Cool blue exotic garden and lily pond laid out following Islamic tradition.

Cimetière
Cimetière Sidi Ahmed Es Zaw Ya
Cimetière Sidi Bel Abbès
NORTHERN MEDINA 59-74
DOUAR AÏN ITTI
Oued Issil
DIOUR JDAD
City Walls and Gates
Cimetière de Sidi Mahta Ben Salah
BAB DOUKKALA
Medersa Ben Youssef
TANNERIES
Almoravid Koubba
Musée de Marrakech
BAB AYLEN
Souks
BEN SALAH
MOUASSINE
NTRAL MEDINA
-40
LA MÉDINA
Night Market
Jemaa El Fna
Koutoubia Mosque
ardins Koutoubia
Dar Si Saïd
Agdal Bab Hmad
UTHERN MEDINA
-58
Maison Tiskiwin
Palais de la Bahia
Cimetière de Bab Ghemat
DI MIMOUN
Palais El Badii
LA MELLAH
Cimetière de Sidi Es Soheili
Tombeaux Saâdiens
KASBAH
Tizi-n-Test, Tiz-n-Tichka, Ourika Valley
Jardins de l'Agdal

Jardin Ménara ▷ 84–85 Romantic pavilion and lake with mountain backdrop.

Jardins de l'Agdal ▷ 45 Royal retreat dotted with lakes and fruit trees–the perfect escape.

Jemaa el Fna ▷ 24–25 Visit the main square to buy, dine and to be entertained.

Koutoubia Mosque ▷ 26–27 Right at the spiritual and physical heart of the city.

Maison Tiskiwin ▷ 48 This house has a lovely little collection of Berber artefacts and all labels are in English.

La Mamounia ▷ 46 Eat, drink and play at this historic hotel and gardens.

Medersa Ben Youssef ▷ 66–67 Beautiful Koranic school and one of the rare religious sights open to non-Muslims.

Musée de Marrakech ▷ 68 Interesting exhibits are outshone by the museum's exquisite interior.

Musée d'Art Islamique ▷ 86 A charming little collection of local art and artefacts.

La Mellah ▷ 47 Wander the labyrinthine streets of this historic district, the Jewish Quarter.

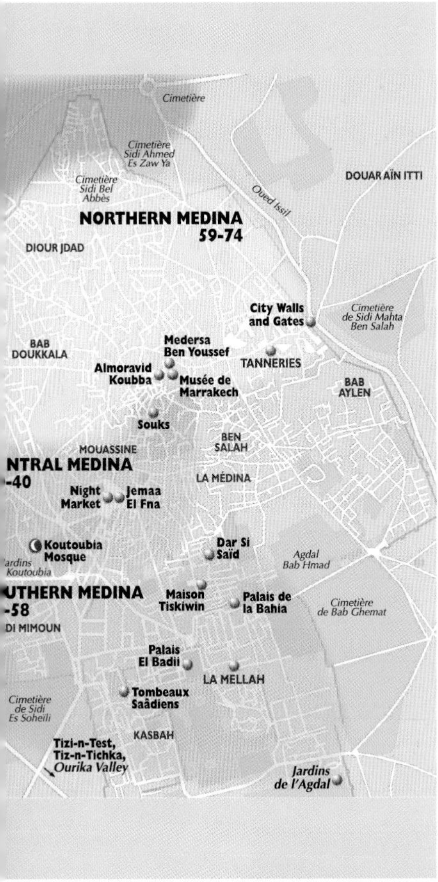

Shopping

Marrakech began as a desert trading post and market place; a role that has taken on international dimensions in recent years. Shopping here is 'major' and personal shoppers can be hired at non-celebrity prices. Gone are the days, though, when a guide was advisable to take you through the maze of the souks. Thanks to a government crackdown and ever present plain-clothed tourist police, stallholders give visitors a relatively easy time. And besides, with any guide you will pay 30 per cent over the odds for any purchase.

From Souks to Malls

The souks sell all kinds of goods and are an enormous, exotic shoppers' playground. Guéliz in the New City couldn't be more different, with bright little boutiques selling contemporary designer takes on traditional goods. Modern, billion-dollar shopping malls and international chain stores are sprouting up in the New City. Their fixed prices can be a real relief after hard bargaining in the souks.

Portable Presents

Babouches (traditional slippers) are ubiquitous and an obvious gift; for something a bit quirky go for the yellow, pointed-toe version. Make two important checks for quality: They should be stitched (not glued) and leather rather than plastic. Tea glasses are another practical and portable purchase. Look for hand-painted rather than machine-decorated and use them at home as pretty candle or pen holders. Natural soaps, whether delicately perfumed

DRIVING A HARD BARGAIN

When shopping in the souks, follow these tips. Don't show how much you like something. Decide a price you are willing to pay before engaging with a stallholder. Offer less than you are prepared to pay and work your way up, slowly and patiently, ignoring any protests. Most importantly, keep smiling. It's all a game.

Shopping in the souks and shops of Marrkech reveals all manner of interesting traditional items

rose, jasmine or almond, provide a daily, sweet-smelling memento of your trip for you or someone back at home.

A Crafty Purchase

Marrakech is awash with crafts for sale. Artisan jewellery could be anything from tribal Berber pieces made from antique silver to colourful ethnic beads. Some of the most stylish hotels in the world now display the huge silver candle lanterns found in almost every riad in Marrakech. If you decide you want one too, make sure to wrap the glass properly when packing. Marrakech is a mecca for leather, whether you are after a fuchsia pouf or a camel skin handbag. Tagines are everywhere, but the decorative pots are only for serving; for an ovenproof tagine get the terracotta version. *Jellabahs* (traditional, long caftans with pointed hoods), while not everyday wear, can be bought in wool for winter, in linen for the heat or even in camouflage for clubbing. The candy-striped handles on Touareg spoons are a work of art from these nomads of the Sahara.

Buying in Bulk

Consider the cost of transporting them home, before you buy bulkier items. Carpets don't necessarily need to be sent back separately; shopkeepers know how to fold them to form a compact parcel for the plane. Shopping for antiques is a minefield; there are few bargains and authenticity can be difficult to verify: buy something because you like it.

TIME TO BUY

Shopping hours are a moveable feast in Marrakech and differ greatly depending on whether you are in the New City or in the medina. The souks and market stalls are generally open Saturday to Thursday 8/9am until 8/ 9pm, Fri 12 until 8, with the stalls close to Jemaa El Fna open until midnight. Most of the shops in the New City are closed Sundays and from around 1pm until 3.30pm, staying open until around 7.30pm..

Shopping by Theme

Marrakech offers frivolous souvenirs, colourful textiles and traditionally made crafts. On this page shops and market stalls are listed by theme. For a more detailed write-up, see the individual listings in Marrakech by Area.

ART AND ANTIQUES

Galerie Damgaard
  (▷ 106)
La Porte d'Or (▷ 74)
La Qoubba (▷ 74)

BOUTIQUES

Ayas (▷ 57)
Intensité Nomade (▷ 90)
Klfkif (▷ 74)
Kulchi (▷ 74)
Michele Baconnier
  (▷ 90)
Mysha and Nito (▷ 90)
Place Vendome (▷ 90)

CRAFTS

Mohamed Bounmentel
  (▷ 57)
Music Shop (▷ 36)
Mustapha Blaoui (▷ 74)

GOVERNMENT CRAFT CENTRES

Centre Artisanal (▷ 54, 57)
Ensemble Artisanal (▷ 33)

HOMEWARE

Côté Sud (▷ 90)
L'Orientaliste (▷ 90)
Original Design (▷ 57)
Scenes de Lin (▷ 90)
Chez Les Nomades
  (▷ 36)
Couleurs Orientales
  (▷ 36)
Herman (▷ 36)
Maison Rouge (▷ 90)

FAIR TRADE

Al Kawtar (▷ 36)
Argan Oil Cooperatives
  (▷ 106)

FOOD

Jeff de Bruges (▷ 90)
Olive Stalls Souk Ableuh
  (▷ 36)

JEWELLERY

Bazaar Atlas (▷ 90)
Grand Bijouterie (▷ 57)

MARKETS

Mellah Market (▷ 57)
Bab Doukkala (▷ 74)

STALLS IN THE SOUK

Akbar Delights (▷ 36)
Beldi (▷ 36)
Boutique Bel Hadj (▷ 36)
Fibule le Sud de Sahara
  (▷ 36)
Souk des Babouches (▷ 74)

ESSSENTIAL MARRAKECH SHOPPING

Marrakech by Night

Nightlife in Marrakech is polarized. In the medieval medina it is almost impossible to get an alcoholic drink (outside of a hotel) because it is illegal to drink in sight of a mosque. In the New City and beyond European clubs are hotbeds of drinking and dancing that would put many international cities to shame.

Night Market

One of the biggest attractions in Marrakech is the Night Market in Jemaa El Fna, a huge, open-air restaurant, with stalls selling delicious Moroccan-style fast food. A meal here is a must on any trip, not least for the entertainment. At dusk storytellers and snake charmers fill the square, joined by boy boxers, traditional musicians and transvestite dancers.

Bright Lights

Both the Koutoubia Mosque and the city walls around the medina are dramatically lit at night. Walk through the Koutoubia Gardens after dark to see the spiritual centre of Marrakech under the spotlight. Dusk is a good time to take a *calèche* (horse-drawn carriage) ride, when the traffic has died down and the city walls are lit up.

All Singing All Dancing

Many Moroccan set menus in restaurants are accompanied by traditional musicians and belly dancers of varying quality. Thoroughly modern Le Comptoir Darna (▷ 92) offers à-la-carte with bellydancing and puts on a good show.

From the top: Koutoubia Mosque at night; casino sign, Hivernage; alfresco dining; bar at Comptoir

INTO THE 21ST CENTURY

In the area of La Palmeraie international entrepreneurs are clearing scrubland to make way for huge resorts, casinos and night clubs—part of the young king's plans to bring Morocco into the 21st century. He hopes this will bring employment and improved living conditions to his people, many of whom are illiterate and living well below the poverty line. This area more than any other is Marrakech at its most modern.

ESSSENTIAL MARRAKECH   MARRAKECH BY NIGHT

13

Eating Out

Gourmands worldwide devour Moroccan cookbooks, and the country's food is served in some of the best restaurants around the globe. In Marrakech a new breed of chef—a group that includes French masters with Michelin stars—are bringing haute cuisine to this desert outpost.

A Home Cooked Meal

Try to eat at least once in a riad—they generally offer family-style cooking that is much better than restaurant food. Many are open to non-guests, but in all cases reservations should be made a day in advance. Many riads also offer small, casual cookery classes that are highly recommended.

Melting Pot

Moroccan food is a direct result of its cultural influences and Marrakech—as a centre for trade and a target for imperialists—is its culinary core. French colonialism lingers in sophisticated dishes; while the staples of couscous, tagines (traditional cooking pots and also the stew in which they are cooked) and *harira* (spicy garlic, chickpea and tomato soup) are testament to Berber origins. The nomads brought dates, milk and bread, while the Andalusian influence can be tasted in lemons, olives and olive oil. From the east the Arabs introduced saffron, coriander, cumin and paprika—adding the touch of spice predominant in so many dishes.

Kif-Kif (Same Same)

Set meals—usually salads, *pigeon pastilla* (pie), tagine with couscous and Moroccan pastries— are annoyingly the only option in many tourist restaurants. While a few of the best can be an approximation of a real Moroccan feast, visitors can find it a drawn-out, expensive and unsatisfying experience and few would want to eat more than one on a single trip to Marrakech. À la carte Moroccan, Asian and international restaurants can all be found too, so concentrate on those.

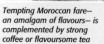

Tempting Moroccan fare— an amalgam of flavours— is complemented by strong coffee or flavoursome tea

Restaurants by Cuisine

Marrakech has restaurants to suit all tastes and all pockets. On this page, they are listed by cuisine. For a more detailed description of each restaurant, see Marrakech by Area.

ESSSENTIAL MARRAKECH IF YOU LIKE...

If You Like...

Whatever your interests, these suggestions will help you get the most out of a trip to the city. All of these sights or listings has a full description in Marrakech by Area.

STYLISH SHOPPING

Treat your home to something from the lovely little shop in the New City, Côté Sud (▷ 90).
Indulge in some fashion Moroccan style in the tiny, famous boutique of Beldi (▷ 36).
Brighten up your kitchen and pick up some eye-catching, coloured ceramics for your table at Original Design (▷ 57).

ROMANTIC RETREATS

Dine in the tropical garden surrounded by birdsong in the wonderful Riad Enija (▷ 112).
Enjoy a steam bath for two and your own private barbecue at exclusive Riad Farnatchi (▷ 112).
Get a room on the rooftop and don't rise 'til noon for a lovely, leisurely breakfast at Riad Tizwa (▷ 111).

Something for everyone— shopping, dining or exotic nightlife

DELICIOUS LOCAL FOOD

Dine on excellent, bargain-priced Moroccan dishes at old favourite, Chez Chegrouni (▷ 38).
Feast on fresh, fast food like fish, spicy sausages or even snails at the atmospheric Night Market (▷ 28–29).
Eat like a king, devouring dish after dish of carefully prepared food, serenaded by traditional music at Le Tobsil (▷ 76).

TRADITIONAL ENTERTAINMENT

Be entertained eastern style by the exotic Belly dancers at Le Comptoir Darna (▷ 92).
Take a short cookery course and learn how to cook authentic Moroccan food with Souk Cuisine (▷ 37).
Be Lawrence of Arabia for a day, riding a camel at Dunes & Desert Exploration (▷ 91).

souvenir drums; Koutabia
Mosque (below)

LUXURIOUS LIVING

Have a private spa at Les Bains de Marrakech (▷ 58).
Go for dinner and dancing at Pacha, the largest nightclub in North Africa, imported from Ibiza (▷ 91).
Follow in the footsteps of kings and celebrities and play a few holes at the Royal Golf Course (▷ 91).

SOUVENIR HUNTING

Stock up with traditional crafts—slippers, lanterns and leather goods—from the souks (▷ 30–31).
Pick up something chic such as a bag or shawl from Kifkif (▷ 74).
Splurge on fine antiques at the upmarket emporium of La Porte d'Or (▷ 74).

SOMETHING FOR FREE

Marvel at the splendour of the Koutoubia Mosque and gardens (▷ 26–27).
Be hypnotized by exotic snake charmers in the main square of Jemaa El Fna (▷ 24–25).
Phone Home or at least email the family, from the strange Moulay Abdeslam Cyber Parc (▷ 75, 115)—an open-air internet café in lush green gardens.

Be mesmorized by
snakes or the DJ's beat

COSMOPOLITAN NIGHTLIFE

Chill out to the international DJ in the bar that is part of the restaurant Le Palais Jad Mahal (▷ 92).
Dance to thumping techno at night

club Theatro (▷ 91) in the plush interior of the former theatre.

Enjoy cocktails, theatre performances and even karaoke at one of the newest clubs, Coleur Pourpre (▷ 91).

A LAZY DAY

Have a scrub, massage and hammam (traditional steam bath) at Les Bains Ziani (▷ 58).
Relax by the pool, lounging with a cocktail or a glass of champagne at Nikki Beach (▷ 91).
Sample café culture with a coffee or even a cocktail at Grand Café de la Poste (▷ 93).

SOMETHING FOR YOUR CHILDREN

Join in the drumming and dancing that takes place nightly in the main square of Jemaa El Fna (▷ 24–25).
Cool down with one of the many flavours of ice cream at Ice Legend (▷ 40).
Take to the water with slides and a wave pool at Oasiria Water Park (▷ 91).

Plenty of fun all round

EXOTIC GARDENS

Relax among soaring palms and leafy banana trees in the tropical garden of Jardin Majorelle (▷ 82–83).
See the snowy Atlas mountains reflected in the pool at Jardin Ménara (▷ 84–85).
Visit the oldest gardens in Marrakech, the 12th-century desert oasis that is Jardins de l'Agdal (▷ 45).

Enjoy the peace at the Jardin Ménara

LOCAL ARCHITECTURE

Gasp at the beauty of the courtyards and galleries of Medersa Ben Youssef (▷ 66–67).
Imagine the splendour at the ancient and enormous complex of royal Palais de Badii (▷ 50–51).
Be dwarfed by the medieval city walls and gates (▷ 65).

Marvel at the detail in the Palais El Badii

This is the heart of the city and covers a compact area including Jemaa El Fna square and its immediate surroundings, as far as the Koutoubia Mosque. Despite its size, this part of Marrakech is packed full of enough sights, sounds and experiences to keep anyone occupied for days.

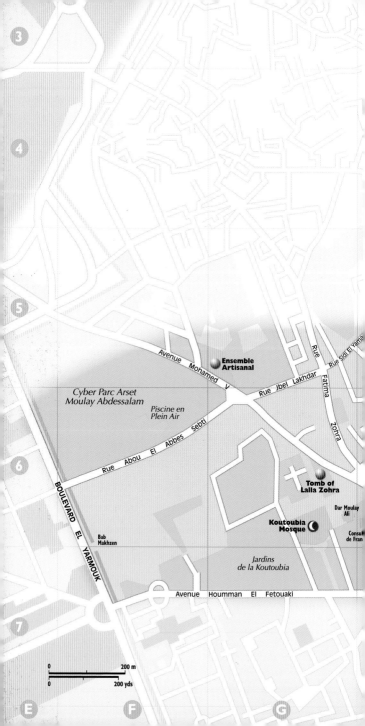

3

4

5

Avenue Mohamed V

Ensemble Artisanal

Rue Jbel Lakhdar

Rue Fatima

Rue Sidi El Yama

Cyber Parc Arset Moulay Abdessalam

Piscine en Plein Air

Zohra

Rue Abou El Abbes Sebti

6

BOULEVARD EL YARMOUK

Bab Makhzen

✠

Tomb of Lalla Zohra

Koutoubia Mosque ☾

Dar Moulay Ali

Consu de Fran

Jardins de la Koutoubia

Avenue Houmman El Fetouaki

7

| 0 | | 200 m |
| 0 | | 200 yds |

E

F

G

Rue El Ksour

MOUASSINE

Zaouia Moul
El Ksour

Haram
Chikh

Souks

Mosquée
Sidi Ishak

Sidi Ishak

Rue Souk Essemarine

Place Rabba
Kédima

Souk Quessabine

Rue Derb Dabachi

**Place Bab
Ftouh**

Koutoubia

Commissariat

Mosquée
Kharbouch

Rue des
Banques

Rue Kennaria

**Night
Market**

**Jemaa
El Fna**

**Café de
France**

**Calèche
Rides**

Poste
Médina

Place
Foucauld

Rue Riad Zitoun El Kédim

Rue de Bab Agnaou

Rue Moulay Ismail

lace Youssef
en Tachfine

Riads Zitoun

Rue Riad Zitoun El Jedid

H   J

Jemaa El Fna

TOP 25

HIGHLIGHTS

- Orange juice stalls
- Snake charmers
- *Gnawa* musicians

TIPS

- Most of the performers do not show up until dusk.
- Bring change for the entertainers who rely on such tips.
- Photographs of anyone from the water sellers to the snake charmers must be paid for, too.
- Ignore the monkey handlers who do not look after their chained animals.

Art, drama and religion are played out here in front of the watchful eyes of visitors every evening. Hypnotized, they sit and watch the captivating spectacle of fortune-tellers, garishly garbed water sellers brandishing copper cups, medicine men and tooth pullers.

Assembly of the Dead city Although Jemaa El Fna means 'Assembly of the Dead', all teeming life is here and the square acts as circus space, health centre and boxing ring. As well as snake charmers, acrobats and cruelly chained monkeys, there are storytellers—who are, quite literally, part of a dying breed. Hennae tattooists—invariably women—are among the most insistent and sinister of sellers, hunched beneath umbrellas, their syringes poised to create their designs.

Clockwise from far left: crowds gather for a performance at Jemaa El Fna; colourful water seller; a storyteller draws a small audience; traditional Berber dancers; a view of the food stalls; drummer and snake charmer; arriving at Jemaa El Fna

World Heritage Site UNESCO recognized Jemaa El Fna as a 'Masterpiece of the Oral and Intangible Heritage of Humanity' in 2001. It soon became pedestrianized to protect its continued existence as an impromptu cultural centre, but it is still often necessary to dodge donkeys and mopeds and the occasional sleeping snake. This is authentic entertainment and not set up for the benefit of tourists.

Food and drink Orange juice sellers hawk their wares from brightly painted wagons. Oranges are cheap and juicy and the juice is squeezed before your eyes. Pick a stallholder that is friendly, and don't let them overcharge you (prices should be clearly displayed). At dusk a whole different story unfolds when the Night Market (▷ 28–29) kicks off and thousands of hungry visitors throng the square.

THE BASICS

🔂 H6
🕐 24 hours
🍴 Café de France (▷ 32)
💷 Free

25

Koutoubia Mosque

HIGHLIGHTS

● The minaret and its architectural details
● Foundations of original mosque
● Koutoubia gardens

TIPS

● Friday prayers at around noon are the most important of the week. Visit then to see the square in front of the mosque fill with devotees.
● Facing the mosque, turn left under the archway for a photo of a towering palm tree.

The splendid, 12th-century minaret of the Koutoubia mosque towers above the square of Jemma El Fna. Spiritual symbol and city landmark, this mosque (entry forbidden to non-Muslims) is at the religious and physical heart of Marrakech.

Call to prayer A constant presence in Marrakech, the Koutoubia mosque's resounding *Adhan* (call to prayer) echoes throughout the city by day, and by night it is spectacularly lit up. At the top of the 69m (226ft) high minaret are the loudspeakers that broadcast the *Adhan*. At many mosques, the call is pre-recorded, but here the call is recited live by the *muezzin* (prayer caller). From an adjacent pole, pointing to Mecca, a flag was traditionally hoist to signal the time for worship, and is still used today if the loudspeakers fail.

Stunning views of the Koutoubia Mosque by day and night

In history The Koutoubia (booksellers') mosque was named for the market stallholders who sold their religious manuscripts nearby as early as the 7th century. The foundations of the first building, built around 1150 by the Almohad dynasty, can still be seen through the railings next to the current mosque. Directly in front of the mosque are two glass enclosures covering the original washing areas. Here, men and women would separately wash their hands, feet and face before entering the mosque.

In the garden Surrounding the mosque are the Koutoubia Gardens, which make for a pleasant stroll (▷ 35). Filled with roses, orange trees and birdsong, ice cream vendors sell their wares to locals relaxing on benches in the shade. It a pleasant place to take a break from the hectic city.

THE BASICS

+ G6
✉ Avenue Bab Jedid
☎ No phone
👁 View from outside
🍴 Café Koutoubia (▷ 40)
✋ No admission to non-Muslims
❓ The call to prayer occurs five times a day between dawn and dusk, but not at set times

Night Market

HIGHLIGHTS

● Melt in your mouth squid, spicy sausages and kebabs
● The chance to experiment; with such prices you can be adventurous
● The lively banter of the stallholders

TIPS

● Don't forget to tip–out of sight and away from the grasp of the greedy owners.
● If you are worried about your tummy, go for fried or boiled food and avoid salad.

Dine beneath a thousand stars, and beside a thousand other customers, surrounded by fortune tellers and snake charmers in one of the largest open air restaurants in the world.

Atmospheric Every night at dusk, as the sun begins to set behind the Koutoubia Mosque (▷ 26–27), gas lanterns are lit and smoke from more than 100 barbecues begins to fill the air of Jemaa El Fna (▷ 24–25). This is just part of the atmospheric medieval pageant where darting boxers and dancing transvestites fill the wings.

Fast food Everyone should eat at the Night Market at least once. The food is fresh, usually either boiled or fried, and reports of illness are extremely rare. This is Moroccan fast food at its

The amzaing atmosphere of the Night Market

best: Just look and point and a delicious meal will be on your table in minutes.

Come ons 'Starvin' like Marvin?' or 'Fish and Chips?' are some of the come-ons you will hear from the multi-lingual stallholders. If it's your first time the 'hustle' can be intimidating, but it's all in good fun, and undercover tourist police ensure restraint. 'Welcome to my air-conditioned restaurant…Five Michelin stars' might be a joke, but these entrepreneurs offer some of the most memorable meals anywhere in Morocco.

On the menu Some stalls have menus in English and French or may specialize in just one dish, such as hard-boiled eggs or bowls of snails. Don't miss the delicious starter of bread and hot tomato dip.

THE BASICS

➕ H6
✉ Jemaa El Fna
☎ No phone
🕐 Daily 6pm–midnight
🍴 Inexpensive

Souks

TOP
25

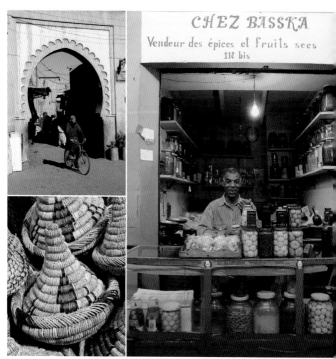

HIGHLIGHTS

● Locally made crafts
● Getting lost in the maze
● Sipping mint tea with the stallholder

TIPS

● Don't say you will come back later. You will probably never find that stall again.
● Think hard before you buy. Many people find themselves having to pay for overweight luggage, or that their tea glasses or lanterns have broken on the route home.

Stretching from the north of Jemaa El Fna all the way to Medersa Ben Youssef are these crowded, chaotic market stalls. Deep Aladdin's caves, they are a highlight whether you want to shop or not; just be prepared to get lost.

A maze This tight, dark web of street bazaars continue to be the very lifeblood of the city that began as a desert trading post. Wander down these densely packed alleyways bustling with donkey carts and mopeds. Here, it is possible to pass 100 cupboard-sized stalls in as many metres, watched by as many pairs of eyes.

How to buy Window-shopping is almost impossible anywhere in the souks, but no one can force you to buy. Do consider what you would pay for

Gateway to the Souk Talaa (far left); grass tagines (far left below); Mohamed Basska's olive and pickle stall (left middle); dried roses and herbs (left below); dyed silks hanging out to dry in the Souk Teinturies (right below); intricate plaster work by an expert carver in the Souk Talaa (bottom)

an item, never show how much you like something and initially offer a third of what you want to pay. Keep a sense of humour, accept some mint tea and remember you are dealing with some of the best salesmen in the world.

Specialist souks Rue Souk Essemarine forms a spine running down the middle, lined with stall-holders hawking *babouches* (traditional slippers), painted tea glasses and brightly coloured leather pouffs aimed at tourists. Traditionally each souk had its own specialty. In the northern reaches are aromatic spice stalls and carpenters' and black-smiths' workshops. Souk des Teinturiers is the dyers' souk, full of photogenic brightly coloured wool while Criée Berbère, once the slave market, now sells carpets. The stalls around Jemaa El Fna offer over-priced, poorer quality goods.

THE BASICS

➕ J5
✉ Central Medina
☎ No phone
🕐 Sat–Thu 9–8, Fri 12–8, with the stalls close to Jemaa El Fna open until midnight
🍴 Café des Épices
❓ Ask a shopkeeper if you get lost (ignore young touts on the street). Since government crackdowns on pushy salesmen, guides are no longer needed, they will certainly add on 30 per cent commission to any purchase

More to See

CAFÉ DE FRANCE

This French café is open long hours. Start the day here with a strong coffee to brace yourself for the souks or sightseeing; return in the evening for a (non-alcoholic) nightcap before retiring. The slightly scruffy rattan chairs, portly waiters and ancient ceiling fans preserve this café's faintly colonial air. The throngs of Jemaa El Fna are within touching distance of the pavement terrace. Some hardened coffee drinkers spend the whole day in the café, but the small, half-heartedly air-conditioned restaurant is not recommended. The two unassuming upper terraces tend to be less crowded spots than Café Argana (▷ 38) or Café Glacier (▷ 40) from which to see the Night Market (▷ 28–29).

🚩 J6 ⊠ Place Jemaa El Fna ☎ No phone
🕐 8am–midnight ✋ Free

CALÈCHE RIDES

Taking a trip in one of these green, canopied horse-drawn carriages may immediately make you stand out as a tourist, but they can be a fun way to travel. For up to five people, they can be used for a sightseeing tour or to travel to sights such as the Jardin Majorelle (▷ 82–83). Increasingly heavy traffic diminishes the romantic element, unless you manage to take a trip in the evening, but children seem to enjoy these novelty rides and it's a memorable way to circle the city walls (▷ 65) and get a good view of what's going on. Although the government introduced fixed hourly prices, it is almost impossible to get drivers to keep to them. Do be prepared to bargain and always agree a price beforehand.

🚩 H6 ⊠ Place Foucauld ☎ No phone
🕐 8am–midnight ✋ Expensive

Jemaa El Fna seen from the Café de France

A calèche *waiting to take a ride*

ENSEMBLE ARTISANAL

Craft production is big business in Marrakech. Although this government-run craft complex is rather ramshackle, it does allow visitors to see craftsmen at work and the prices are (mostly) fixed. Although not as slick or as comprehensive as its sister store, Centre Artisanal (▷ 54, 57), this collection of artisan items is more central and less claustrophobic with a pleasing courtyard and café. For larger items you will usually pay a third more than at market stalls, but without the often tortuous bargaining process. Smaller items are often roughly the same price and generally of better quality than those in the souks—where you should watch out for plastic slippers sold as leather, for example. Dedicated shoppers come here to check prices before heading off to bargain in the souks, and it is a relaxed place to browse. Watch out for unscrupulous stallholders and shopkeepers who fail to display price tags.

🔛 G5 ✉ Avenue Mohamed V ☎ 024 386 876 🕓 Daily 8.30–7 🍴 Courtyard café 🖐 Free

PLACE BAB FTOUH

Just north of Jemaa El Fna, before you enter the souks, is the small square of Bab Ftouh. Here, tea glass sellers vie for attention with miniature, air-conditioned boutiques. In a little nook on its southern edge are dedicated olives stands, piled high in black and green edible pyramids. In the northwestern corner of Bab Ftouh is Souk Fondouk Ouarzazi. Merchants once travelled across the Sahara from as far away as Timbuktu and the Sudan to trade silks, spices and even slaves in the souks of Marrakech. They slept in the upstairs galleries of the *fondouks* (former inns); the central courtyard accommodating their horses. Some *fondouks* are up to 500 years old and quite literally falling apart, others like Ourzazi have been turned into a kind of Moroccan mini mall for antiques with prices to match Liberty, London's luxury department store.

🔛 H5 ✉ Place Bab Ftouh 🕓 Most stalls are open by 9am and do not pack up until midnight. Closed Friday am 🍴 Café de France (▷ 32)

Souks stall at night at Jemaa El Fna

You can buy handmade felt bags in the Ensemble Artisanal

TOMB OF LALLA ZOHRA

Next to the buzzing traffic of Avenue Mohamed V and standing in the shadow of the Koutoubia Mosque (▷ 26–27), this tomb is easily overlooked. The unassuming, castellated *koubba* (domed mausoleum) is the final resting place of Lalla Zohra—daughter of a 17th-century religious leader. Both a real and mythical figure, Lalla Zohra was said to be a woman by day and a white dove at night. She was worshipped by women both to increase their fertility and to protect their children—who would often be dedicated to her. The windows and door of the mausoleum have long been blocked-up and it is no longer open to the public. Painted icing-white and castellated, the tomb sits humbly on the large open square in front of the soaring Koutoubia Mosque.

🔳 G6 ⊠ Avenue Mohamed V, in front of the Koutoubia Mosque ☎ No phone 🍴 Café de Koutoubia (▷ 40)

The tomb of Lalla Zohra

The Heart of Marrakech

Explore central Marrakech's key points of interest. Begin in Jemaa El Fna (▷ 24–25), encircle the Koutoubia Mosque (▷ 26–27) and gardens and end up on the edge of the souks (▷ 30–31).

DISTANCE: 2km (1 mile)   **ALLOW:** 2 hours including lunch

START   **END**

JEMAA EL FNA   **JEMAA EL FNA**
➕ H6   ➕ H6

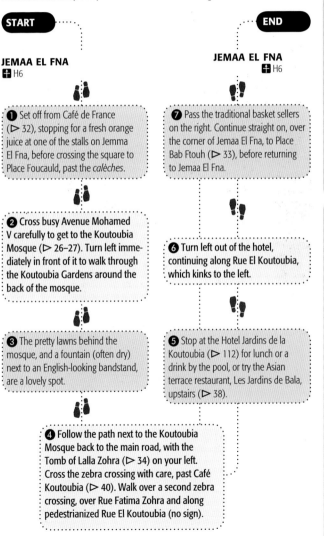

❶ Set off from Café de France (▷ 32), stopping for a fresh orange juice at one of the stalls on Jemma El Fna, before crossing the square to Place Foucauld, past the *calèches*.

❼ Pass the traditional basket sellers on the right. Continue straight on, over the corner of Jemaa El Fna, to Place Bab Ftouh (▷ 33), before returning to Jemaa El Fna.

❷ Cross busy Avenue Mohamed V carefully to get to the Koutoubia Mosque (▷ 26–27). Turn left immediately in front of it to walk through the Koutoubia Gardens around the back of the mosque.

❻ Turn left out of the hotel, continuing along Rue El Koutoubia, which kinks to the left.

❸ The pretty lawns behind the mosque, and a fountain (often dry) next to an English-looking bandstand, are a lovely spot.

❺ Stop at the Hotel Jardins de la Koutoubia (▷ 112) for lunch or a drink by the pool, or try the Asian terrace restaurant, Les Jardins de Bala, upstairs (▷ 38).

❹ Follow the path next to the Koutoubia Mosque back to the main road, with the Tomb of Lalla Zohra (▷ 34) on your left. Cross the zebra crossing with care, past Café Koutoubia (▷ 40). Walk over a second zebra crossing, over Rue Fatima Zohra and along pedestrianized Rue El Koutoubia (no sign).

Shopping

AKBAR DELIGHTS

This tiny shop sells finely embroidered slippers and textiles with an Asian influence that wouldn't be out of place on the Champs-Élysées; prices reflect this.

➕ H5 ✉ 45 Place Bab Ftouh ☎ 071 661 307 🚫 Closed Monday

AL KAWTAR

www.alkawtar.org

This boutique sells fair trade bed and table linens as well as clothing at fixed prices, made at a workshop for disabled women and girls. Only 100 per cent natural fibres are used, all pieces are embroidered, knitted or crocheted by hand and can be made to order.

➕ H5 ✉ 57 Rue El Ksour ☎ 024 378 293

BELDI

Upmarket boutique selling at European prices at the entrance to the medina. On sale is tailoring by two brothers in desirable fabrics with a contemporary flair.

➕ H5 ✉ 9–11 Rue El Ksour ☎ 024 441 076

BOUTIQUE BEL HADJ

Tucked up in the top of this *fondouk*, the owner, Bari, presides over his treasure trove of jewellery—much of it tribal—from as far away as China, Nepal and the Ivory Coast. Again, don't expect bargains.

➕ H5 ✉ Souk fondouk el Ouarzazi 22–23 (upstairs) ☎ 024 441 258

CHEZ LES NOMADES

www.chezlesnomades.com

Colourful rugs from the Atlas Mountains and around are on sale here where the 'language' of Moroccan rugs and the motifs used can be explained in English. The website details some of the varied pieces, where orders can be made online. These rugs make great presents.

➕ J5 ✉ 32–34 Bradia El Kédima, Mouassine ☎ 024 442 259

COULEURS ORIENTALES

This little place selling brightly coloured items in lovely fabrics at fixed prices would not be out of place in the New City. Visit for funky foot and home wear.

➕ J6 ✉ 233 Rue Riad Zitoun El Jedid ☎ No phone

A HARD BARGAIN

The stalls around Jemaa El Fna are well used to tourists who can't face the mayhem of the souks. If you do decide to buy anything here, bear in mind that prices are often double what they would be even meters away, and the stallholders are much harder to bargain with. Also, take note, the quality of the goods is often poorer.

FIBULE LE SUD DE SAHARA

The smiling owner of this little shop selling Berber and Touareg jewellery dresses true to his Touareg roots in a bright blue kaftan and turban.

➕ H5 ✉ Souk fondouk el Ouarzazi 27 (upstairs) ☎ 070 965 273

HERMAN

Authentic, earthenware (which are ovenproof) tagines are on sale at this little place off the main square. There are decorative, ceramic versions, too, but these are for serving purposes only.

➕ H7 ✉ 3 Rue Moulay Ismail ☎ No phone

MUSIC SHOP

This little place is filled with traditional instruments from hand-held drums to tambourines. They make unusual souvenirs for budding musicians or even just to decorate your home.

➕ J6 ✉ 84 Rue Riad Zitoun El Jedid ☎ No phone

OLIVE STALLS SOUK ABLEUH

In a little nook just off Jemaa El Fna, is a small cluster of stalls specializing in olives of all colours and flavours. Try a handful of green olives with chilli, or plump black ones with lemon. The preserved lemons make good presents.

➕ H5 ✉ Near Place Bab Ftouh ☎ No phone

Entertainment and Activities

CAFE ARABE

www.cafearabe.com

One of the few places where you can buy alcohol in the central medina, but this is not the only reason to come to this Italian-owned venue. Excellent cappuccinos and pretty pastries. It's also a sophisticated, candle-lit lounge bar/restaurant with music and decent Italian/Moroccan food. Sip a cocktail on the 1960's inspired terrace sitting on comfortable sofas—a world away from the medieval medina. Tuck into beautifully presented cuisine washed down with fine wines in the restaurant, or simply enjoy a mint tea and homemade cakes in the café.

✚ H5 ✉ 184 Rue Mouassine ☎ 024 429 728

GRAND TAZI HOTEL

This really is the only place around Jemma El Fna to get a cheap beer. Distinctly down-at-heel and haunt of backpackers, there are comfortable chairs and a relaxed atmosphere. There is absolutely nothing grand about this hotel so don't even think of staying here even if you have one too many. The rooms are dirty and the reservation system disorganized.

✚ H7 ✉ Corner of Ave El Mouahidine and Rue de Bab Agnaou ☎ 024 442 787

JARDINS DE LA KOUTOUBIA

www.lesjardinsdelakoutoubia. com

If you lunch at any of the restaurants at this hotel (▷ 112), you can (unless the hotel is full to capacity) use the lovely swimming pool, surrounded by trees and birdsong. For real indulgence—ideally before lunch—make a visit to the hotel spa (bookings essential) for a massage or maybe a facial.

✚ H6 ✉ 26 Rue El Koutoubia ☎ 024 388 800

KSSOUR AGAFAY

www.kssouragafay.com

No doubt this first members' club in the medina is the shape of things to come. As parts of Marrakech become ever more exclusive, accessible to only the rich, fashionable or well-connected, this self-billed 'world-class cultural and international arts centre' will cater to a growing need. Kssour

---

CHARMING

It is easy to be charmed by the magic of Jemaa El Fna just as surely as the snakes in the square. At dusk, join in the dancing, drumming and handclapping of hypnotic *gnawa* performers (bring change for a donation). This traditional Moroccan slave music is entrancing fans of all ages worldwide.

Agafay Town and Country Club is a hotel and spa outside of the city

✚ H5 ✉ 52 Sabet Graoua ☎ 024 427 000

PIANO BAR OUARZAZI

www.lesjardinsdelakoutoubia. com

The snug little corner of this luxury hotel nightly serves very decent cocktails to the tinkling from the resident pianist, creating a not particularly Moroccan—but very pleasant—atmosphere. The service is slick, the drinks strong (although not cheap) and you could easily find yourself whiling away a few hours here either before or after dinner. In fact, don't miss the chance to eat at one of the hotel's excellent restaurants.

✚ H6 ✉ 26 Rue El Koutoubia ☎ 024 388 800

SOUK CUISINE

www.soukcuisine.com

This cookery course is a highly recommended 'taste' of Morocco that offers a real insight into local culture. You will be taken to the market to buy ingredients and then to the owner's house to create traditional Moroccan dishes. The very reasonable price includes lunch and wine and a full day of entertainment. Also on offer are week-long culinary courses.

✚ J5 ✉ Zniknet Rahba, 5 Derb Tahtah ☎ 073 804 955

Restaurants

PRICES

Prices are approximate,
based on a 3-course
meal for one person.
€€€   over €40
€€   €20–€40
€   under €20

CAFÉ ARGANA (€€)

The food is mediocre at
best, with often surly service, but it's worth ordering
for the bird's-eye view of
the Night Market from the
third floor terrace. Non-
diners get firmly relegated
to the back.
✚ H6 ✉ Jemaa El Fna
☎ No phone 🕐 Daily 12–12

CHEZ BAHIA (€)

This little Moroccan eatery
dishes up hearty tagines,
bubbling soups and
colourful salads. A real
locals' place that is completely unpretentious and
consistently good quality.
✚ J6 ✉ Rue Riad Zitoun
El Kédim ☎ No phone
🕐 Daily 11–8

CHEZ CHEGROUNI (€)

It's hard to fault this simple, long-standing place
serving kebabs, chips,
salad and soups. A recent
face-lift means no more
writing orders on a napkin
before settling down in
the mosaic-lined interior
or on the carved wooden
terrace.
✚ J6 ✉ Jemaa El Fna
☎ 024 654 746
🕐 Daily 7am–11pm

CLUB MED LA MEDINA (€€€)

www.clubmed.co.uk
It's a bit of a secret that
this exclusive enclave
catering to a predomi-
nantly French clientele
is open to non-residents
for both a themed, varied
buffet and a very good
lunch. One night there
could be a seafood buf-
fet, the next a Moroccan
or international theme,
but the food is of a
consistently high stand-
ard. Reservations advised.
✚ H6 ✉ Jemaa El Fna
☎ 024 444 016 🕐 Daily
1–3, 8–9.30

DAR ES SALAM (€€)

www.dares-salam.com
There are five lounges
here—the 17th-century
K'dim lounge was the set-
ting for Alfred Hitchcock's
*The Man who Knew too
Much*. This is the main

LIKE BEES TO HONEY

Rather like London's
Leicester Square, or Time
Square in New York, the
main square of Jemaa El Fna
is a honeypot for tourists.
Drawing thousands of international visitors every day,
it is a hotbed for tourist rip-
offs. Generally, food is more
expensive here and it is easy
to get a bad, and expensive,
meal. Follow these recom-
mendations, some of which,
as described, should be
visited for their viewpoints as
much as the food.

attraction, not the mediocre set menu.
✚ H5 ✉ 170 Rue Riad
Zitoun El Kédim ☎ 024 443
520 🕐 Daily 12.30–3, 8–12

LES JARDINS DE BALA (€€)

www.lesjardinsdelakoutoubia.
com
Although billed as Indian
food, the dishes here,
such as vegetarian stir-
fries and tapas, have a
distinctly Asian—even
European—bent. Attentive
service and a rooftop with
a wonderful view of the
mosque are major draws.
✚ H6 ✉ 26 Rue El
Koutoubia ☎ 024 388 800
🕐 Daily 12–3.30, 7.30–12

LES JARDINS DE LA KOUTOUBIA (€€)

www.lesjardinsdelakoutoubia.
com
Pool-side, light French
and international lunch,
with excellent service
accompanied by bird-
song, is a much better
option than the some-
times stuffy, although very
good, restaurant in the
evenings. Dishes include
excellent salads and
steaks, and delicious ice
cream and sorbets; and
the service is charming
and efficient.
✚ H6 ✉ 26 Rue El
Koutoubia ☎ 024 38 88 00
🕐 Daily 12–4

NIGHT MARKET (€)

Consistently excellent
food such as spicy sau-
sages, fish and chips,
delicately fried crispy

squid, and vegetable kebabs is dished up here with bread and spicy sauce. This freshly cooked food is as good as you will get anywhere in Morocco.

🔝 H6 ✉ Jemaa El Fna ☎ No phone 🕐 Daily 6pm–12

PIZZERIA VENEZIA (€€)

Very good pasta, pizza and salads are on offer here, although there's no alcohol due to the proximity to Koutoubia Mosque. There are great views at sunset from the breezy terrace.

🔝 G6 ✉ 279 Avenue Mohamed V ☎ 024 440 081 🕐 Daily 12–3, 6.30–11.30

PORTOFINO RISTORANTE PIZZERIA (€€)

This low-lit Italian restaurant looks rather like a pizzeria chain and is popular with Westerners. But there is much more than just pizza; pasta and salads, even prawn cocktail and tiramisu, as well as dishes featuring beef and seafood, are on the menu.

🔝 G6 ✉ 279 Avenue Mohamed V ☎ 024 391 665 🕐 Daily 12–11 or 12

RESTAURANT AL BARAKA (€€)

www.albaraka.to
Traditional Moroccan food—pigeon pastilles, chicken tagines and vegetable couscous, with a set menu in the evening accompanied by music and dancing. Eat in the salon or on the terrace.

🔝 H6 ✉ 1 Place Jemaa El Fna ☎ 024 44 23 41 🕐 Daily 7–11

RESTAURANT MARRAKCHI (€€€)

www.lemarrakchi.com
Admittedly touristy, but eating in this two-storey restaurant overlooking Jemaa El Fna is a memorable experience. Fine wines and Moroccan favourites served in a candle-lit environment filled with the strains of Moroccan music.

🔝 J6 ✉ 52 Rue des Banques ☎ 024 443 377 🕐 Daily noon–1am

RESTAURANT RELAIS DE PARIS (€€)

www.lesjardinsdelakoutoubia.com
This intimate restaurant next to a large swimming pool is an elegant spot.

LICENSE TO SERVE

There are strict rules forbidding alcohol to be served in sight of a mosque. Many a tourist thirsting for a beer to wash down their sausage and chips at the Night Market have cursed the rule. Do respect the local customs, weighted with religious significance, and remember there are a few hidden away places, detailed here, that can satisfy your need for an alcoholic drink.

Rib steak with homemade chips and grilled duck breast are stand outs from the concise menu.

🔝 H6 ✉ 26 Rue El Koutoubia ☎ 024 388 800 🕐 Daily 12–3.30, 7.30–12

LE RIAD DES MERS (€€)

www.ilovemarrakesh.com/riaddesmers
Fresh fish and seafood, such as oysters and lobsters, are brought in daily from the coast, and there are also some Italian favourites, offering welcome relief from traditional tagine fare. This is a friendly place and one of the rare restaurants to serve seafood in the medina.

🔝 F3 ✉ 411 Derb Sidi Messoud ☎ 024 375 304 🕐 Daily 8–12

LES TERRASSES DE L'ALHAMBRA (€–€€)

One of the more comfortable and nicest places to eat on the square, with a simple menu of salads—Niçoise and warm goat's cheese, Morrocan dishes and good, thin-crust pizza. Cooling ice creams and sorbets are available in children's portions. There are three floors here; sit on the upper level for a bit of a breeze and great views of the edge of Jemaa El Fna.

🔝 J6 ✉ Jemaa El Fna ☎ 024 427 570 🕐 Daily 8am–11pm

Cafes, Ice Cream Parlours and Drink Stalls

ARSAT EL BILK (€)

You will find mostly locals here, making a welcome change from tourist laded Jemma El Fna around the corner. They sit here to read, to smoke, to drink coffee and generally watch the world go by. No food.

✚ H6 ✉ Rue Moulay Ismail, opposite Place Foucauld ☎ No Phone ⏰ Daily 9–7

CAFÉ DE FRANCE (▷ 32)

CAFÉ GLACIER (€–€€)

The top floor terrace may be the best vantage point from which to view the Night Market. However, the turn-style entry, compulsory drink purchase and scrum of camera-wielding tourists are decidedly unappealing. Consider visiting during the day instead.

✚ H6 ✉ Hotel CTM, Jemaa El Fna ☎ 024 42 23 25 ⏰ Daily 8am–midnight

CAFÉ DE KOUTOUBIA (€)

The pavement terrace is filled all day with a mix of tourist and local coffee drinkers. Because it is often so busy service can be slow, but it's worth it for the view of Koutoubia Mosque. It's a good spot for people-watching, too, as a constant parade of individuals pass in all directions right in front of the terrace. Drink a cool water or refreshing mint tea as you drink in the view.

✚ G6 ✉ ✉ Rue Fatima Zohra, on corner with Avenue Mohamed V ☎ No phone ⏰ Daily 7–11

ENSEMBLE ARTISANAL CAFÉ (€)

Not worth a special trip, but this courtyard café is very convenient for a shopping stop-gap. Take a break with a mint tea, coffee, or even a Moroccan soup or tagine.

✚ G5 ✉ Avenue Mohamed V ☎ 024 386 876 ⏰ Mon–Sat 10–6

ICE LEGEND (€)

Have a break from the snake charmers and acrobats in the main square, and cool down with a choice of around 40 flavours of ice creams and sorbets to eat in or take away at this popular ice cream parlour. Everything is homemade here and there's always an eager queue. You will find you always want more: this place really is legendary.

✚ H6 ✉ 52 Rue de Bab Agnaou ☎ 024 444 200 ⏰ Daily 9–9

PATISSERIE MIK MAK (€)

Visit this patisserie for breakfast or a sweet snack of cakes or biscuits, as well as juices and ice cream. Stand up at the counter inside or take away. On offer here are both Moroccan and European goodies, along with ice cream, soft drinks and chocolates. Popular with locals who come to indulge themselves with almond juice and home-made yoghurt.

✚ H6 ✉ Avenue Moulay Ismail, next to Hotel Ali ☎ No phone ⏰ Daily 8–7.30

PATISSERIE DES PRINCES (€)

Delicious, melt in the mouth pastries and cakes in this shiny patisserie. French creations, as well as Moroccan, including crêpes, pan chocolat and croissants to eat in or take away. You might find yourself lured by the cool of the air-conditioned interior and find it hard to leave. Be warned though: creations tend to be sweeter versions than European ones, some with unusual fillings. Be prepared to experiment.

✚ H6 ✉ 32 Rue de Bab Agnaou ☎ No Phone ⏰ Daily 8am–11pm

JUICY FRUIT

Drink an orange juice squeezed before your eyes in the shade of the canopy of one of the brightly painted green and orange wagons in Jemaa El Fna. All the numbered stalls are good, so just pick one with your lucky number or by the size of the juice seller's smile.

This is the royal quarter; site of two magnificent ancient palaces and some striking royal tombs. The Agdal Gardens are still used by the royal family but only sporadically and the historic Mellah and the shopping mecca of Centre Artisanal are worth a visit, as well as the glorious Mamounia hotel.

4

5

6

7

Avenue Houmman El Fetouaki

Place Youssef
Ben Tachfine

La Mamounia

Youssef
Ben Tachfine

Rue Lalla Rkia

Rue Ben Naffie

Avenue Houmman El Feto

Rue Ibn Rachid

Rue Rachid

SIDI MIMOUN

Rue Sidi Mimoun

BOULEVARD EL YARMOUK

Rue Arset El Maach

**Kasbah
Mosque**

8

Hôpital
Ibn Zohr

**Bab
Agnaou**

Zaouïa
Sidi Es Soheïli

Cimetière
de Sidi Es Soheïli

**Tombeaux
Saâdiens**

Rue de la Kasbah

**Centre
Artisanal**

9

0   200 m
0   200 yds

KASBA

Rue

F   **G**   **H**

Dar Si
Saïd

Palais
Moulay
Idriss

Rue Riad Zitoun El Jedid

Rue du Djenan Ben Chegra

Préfecture
de la Médina

Rue de la Bahia

Agdal
Bab Hmad

Maison
Tiskiwin

Rue Imam El Ghazali

Rue Riad Zitoun El Kedim

Palais de
la Bahia

Lantern
Workshops

Miâara
(Cimetière Juif)

Rue du Djenan

Bab
Berrima

Place des
Ferblantiers

Palais
El Badii

LA MELLAH

Rue du Djenan El Atia

Rue Berrima

Palais
Royal

Méchouar

Bab
Ahmar

Rue Bab Ahmar

chouar

Jardins
de l'Agdal

J

K

L

Dar Si Saïd

Arab horseshoe door (left) and archway revealing beautful tiles (right), Da Si Saïd

THE BASICS

K6

Derb El Bahia, Rue Riad Zitoun El Jedid

024 442 464

Wed–Mon 9–12.15, 3.15–5.30

The descriptions of the exhibits are in French and Arabic only but a guide can give you an insightful tour (for a small fee) in English

HIGHLIGHTS

● Delicate jewellery in precious metals with gemstones
● The marble Almoravid basin
● Medieval looking wooden fairground swings used up until 1960

The building, with its traditional three floors and central courtyard, is a museum piece in itself, with extraordinary carved ceilings and some pretty gardens. Inside, is an impressive collection of Moroccan decorative arts.

Treasure trove Hidden down a tiny alleyway behind fortress-like walls is this residence made up of two riads and central courtyards filled with citrus trees and flowers. The brother of the man who constructed the Palais de la Bahia (▷ 49) built this late 19th-century palace, which today houses the Museum of Muslim Arts.

Arts and crafts Wooden crafts feature heavily in the museum, particularly intricately carved wood Berber doors, which today are used in many of the more upmarket riads in the medina. Berber wedding chairs can also be seen; they are still made today from wood and used to carry the bride in wedding ceremonies. Daggers, silver and amber jewellery and fine mosaic tiling are also worth looking out for. The star attraction is probably a rectangular basin from the Almoravid period. Brought over from Spain in the 10th century and originally kept in the Medersa Ben Youssef (▷ 66–67), it is surprising that the animal decorations remain (Islam forbids such images) and that the conquering Almohads did not destroy the whole piece. Signs guide visitors through a series of rooms displaying well-marked exhibits.

Having a picnic among the olive trees (right) at the lovely Jardins de l'Agdal (left)

Jardins de l'Agdal

The back garden of the royal palace was built as a royal retreat in the 12th-century, predating even the famed Alhambra Gardens in Spain. Spread over 3sq km (1.2sq miles), with welcome shade provided by orange, apricot, pomegranate and olive trees, they form an orchard oasis in the desert.

Historic changes The word 'Agdal' means 'walled meadow', deriving from the Berber tradition of creating an enclosed pasture close to home. Although the original concept and the larger, huge artificial lake date from the Almohad period when the gardens were created, various changes have taken place over the years. The Saâdiens expanded the plot several times and the present shape of the gardens, as well as the high *pisé* (mud and clay) walls that enclose them, dates from the 19th century.

Desert pools Artificial lakes and a sophisticated watering system were created from subterranean rivers harnessed from the Ourika Valley (▷ 100–101) 30km (19 miles) away. In the 19th century, sultans held extravagant boating parties here, until one drowned when his vessel sank in the lake.

Garden features The Agdal is actually a series of interconnected gardens—the perfect place for a long, reflective walk. As you wander you'll catch glimpses of cooling reservoirs through the trees and find evocative vineyards and orchards.

THE BASICS

🔢 L9

✉ Access is from the path leading from the Méchouar Intérior. (Note: this looks like a road on the map but is a parade ground immediately south of the palace)

🕐 Fri and Sun 8–5.30; closed when the king is in residence

✋ Free

HIGHLIGHTS

● Enjoying a picnic in the shade of the fruit trees
● Panoramic views of the Atlas Mountains and the Koutoubia Mosque

TIPS

● The gardens are not open when the king is in residence, which is usually in winter.
● Instead of walking here, take a taxi and save your energy for a long walk around the gardens.

La Mamounia

The haunt of Winston Churchill and royalty, La Mamounia is deliciously ornate

THE BASICS

www.mamounia.com
F7
Avenue Bab Jedid
024 388 600

HIGHLIGHTS

● A Mamounia cocktail in the Churchill Piano Bar
● Splendid bird-filled gardens, tended by 40 gardeners daily
● Views of the Atlas Mountains from the balconies
● A roll of the dice in the grand old casino
● State of the art sports facilities, including a gym

TIP

● Non-residents can sample a piece of Mamounia history with a visit to one of the bars and restaurants, or even the casino—dress codes apply.

Like the Raffles Hotel in Singapore, or London's Ritz hotel, the Mamounia is one of the greatest hotels in the world. Much more than a place to stay, it evokes the city's golden age.

Living legend Opened in 1923, this art deco hotel with Moorish influences is surrounded by impressive, 300-year-old gardens. It is also home to a casino, part of the rich legend of Marrakech.

Making history La Mamounia will forever be associated with Sir Winston Churchill, who stayed in the hotel during his Marrakech painting jaunts. A suite and the piano bar are named after him. Writing to President Franklin D. Roosevelt, Churchill called it 'the most lovely spot in the whole world'. Anyone who stays here is in good company—royalty and celebrities regularly visit La Mamounia, and the current king even owns a share of the hotel.

Recent renovations Enlarged and renovated many times over the years, at the time of writing the hotel was undergoing its biggest overhaul yet. Interior designer Jacques Garcia, who specializes in bringing historic hotels into the 21st century, had been brought in from Paris. Closed in July 2006, re-opening had been severely delayed, some say due to agonizing over how to best conceive a major reinvention of such an historic landmark. Extensive sporting facilities and a casino add to the new style.

Bab Essalam market (left) and the Star of David tiling (right) in the Jewish Quarter

La Mellah

The once lively, walled Mellah (Jewish Quarter) was home to thousands of Jews. Today, however, only a couple of hundred live in the city, but they still come to worship in the now mainly Muslim Mellah.

Gated communities *Mellahs* are gated Jewish neighbourhoods found throughout Morocco, formed to protect their inhabitants from the Arabs outside. These communities quickly became overcrowded and the impoverished people within became dirty and disease ridden. In Marrakech's La Mellah, very few of the synagogues that were once in every street remain today.

Places of worship It is easy to get lost looking for the synagogues as they are often found at the end of tiny, unmarked alleyways, with no signs at their entrances. The Alzama Synagogue is on one side of a neat courtyard that it shares with local residences and a community centre. Constructed at the turn of the 20th century, a separate gallery that allows women to pray was only added in the 1950s. This modern innovation means female worshippers are no longer left to sit in the entrance or in a separate room. Religious services are held on Fridays and Saturdays.

Market place The Mellah market has been feeding the local population for around 500 years. You don't have to buy anything, just photograph the enormous coloured cones of spices.

THE BASICS

➕ K8
🕐 24 hours; market daily except Fri morning
✋ Free

HIGHLIGHTS

● Synagogues, particularly the Alzama, although you may need a guide to find them
● The Mellah market, (▷ 57), between Place des Ferblantiers and Palais Badii, sells exotic food

Maison Tiskiwin

TOP 25

Saharan wooden figure (left) and Stucco arch (right), both in the Maison Tiskiwin

THE BASICS

✚ J7

✉ 8 Rue de la Bahia, Riads Zitoun

☎ 024 389 192

🕐 Daily 9.30–12.30, 3–6

HIGHLIGHTS

● Dramatic African masks carved out of wood
● Beautifully worked traditional carpets

TIP

● Walk upstairs first so you can follow the room numbers in the booklet.

This museum is a joy for two reasons— the exhibits are well documented in English and because it's so small it tends to be mercifully free of the tour groups that swamp so much in Marrakech.

Humble house Between the rather grand Dar Si Saïd and the Bahia Palace, is this altogether more modest dwelling. Maison Tiskiwin is a town house that belonged to Bert Flint, a Dutch anthropologist who filled it with his treasured private collection of Berber and Saharan artefacts.

Round trip Visitors are handed a detailed, sometimes verbose, booklet in English called 'A Round Trip from Marrakech to Timbuktu', describing the varied displays. Indeed, Morocco, Niger, Mali and Mauritania are all covered in this journey through Africa. The large room in the second courtyard is the private lounge of the owner, containing masks, rugs and furnishings he collected on his travels.

Academic assistance Bert Flint donated the house and the majority of his collection to the city in 2006. While he remains as curator for the museum, it is administered by the University of Marrakech, which has pledged to continue the anthropologist's research work. The current exhibition continues, with a library, study areas and changing events planned for the future.

Intrictate detail and patterning displayed on the remarkable Palais de la Bahia

TOP 25

Palais de la Bahia

On the Northern edge of the Mellah, this palace is a cool retreat from the heat of the streets of the Kasbah and nearby main square of Jemaa El Fna. Delight in the series of paved courtyards and rooms with high, vaulted ceilings.

Humble beginnings Born a black slave, ruthless Grand Vizier (chief advisor to the sultan) Bou Ahmed, built this palace at the end of the 19th century to house his four wives and two-dozen concubines. He named it *Bahia* ('The Brilliant') intending it to rival the finest Moorish palaces, but the traditional upper galleries were omitted due to his debilitating obesity.

Architectural splendour A long courtyard entrance leads to reception halls with vaulted ceilings and female quarters opening on to banana tree and palm filled courtyards. The rooms on view are unfurnished but the architectural detail is impressive: intricately carved stucco panels, finest *zellij* (Moorish mosaic tiling) and honeycombs of gilded cedar.

Interesting associations The Palais de la Bahia is still used as a royal residence and most of the 150 rooms are closed to the public, although in 2001 rap singer P. Diddy filled them with super models and celebrities for a spectacular $1 million dollar party. The writer, Edith Wharton stayed in the favourite wife's room, and in her book, *In Morocco* (1927) remembered the 'flowers and shadows and falling water…'

THE BASICS

➕ K7

✉ Rue de la Bahia, Zitoun El Jedid

🕐 Daily 8.30–12, 2.30–6

♿ Inexpensive

HIGHLIGHTS

● Intricate *zellij* tiling
● Historical, literary and contemporary links
● Imagining the extent and the original use of the extensive building

TIPS

● Tour groups tend to swamp this popular attraction. Either avoid at peak times or hang back to appreciate the tranquil space away from the hoards.
● Although the rooms can seem very similar, take a while to conjure up their unique purpose.

SOUTHERN MEDINA

★

TOP 25

Palais El Badii

HIGHLIGHTS

● Highly decorated *minbar*
● The central court with its now empty basins
● Storks and sparrows on the battlements

TIPS

● At the main entrance buy a double ticket that includes the *minbar* as they can't be purchased inside.
● Don't miss the view from the terrace.
● This sight in particular gets very hot, so try to visit early in the morning.

Originally adorned with marble, onyx and gold, this extravagant palace was built by Saâdien ruler Ahmed El Mansour in 1578. It took 25 years to finish, and just half that for conquering sultan, Moulay Ismail, to strip it bare.

Hole in the wall A hole in the three-storey-high pink dusty walls—all that is left of the gatehouse —leads to an empty courtyard and now dry pool. This enormous complex was once filled with politicians, poets and parties, but today only birdsong and a solitary palm tree greet the visitor.

Bird's-eye view Only the tower on the north-eastern side retains its internal staircase; it leads to a terrace where storks and sparrows have a bird's-eye view as they stand sentinel. A plan in English shows the original layout, including the

Crystal Pavilion for the king, with its own pools and lounge, but only the foundations remain.

Work of art A splash of bright bougainvillea is the only indicator of the extraordinary Koutoubia *minbar* (pulpit), perhaps one of the finest works of art in wood in the world. It is heavily decorated with delicate woodcarving and marquetry, with finely carved frogs and stars and features verses from the Koran about Allah's dominion over heaven and earth.

Spanish skill The *minbar* was shipped over from Córdoba, Spain where it took skilled craftsmen eight years to build. Originally used in the Koutoubia Mosque (▷ 26–27); a sophisticated mechanism allowed it to be wheeled out for the *imam* (priest) to use on Fridays, this medieval masterpiece forming an exquisite 'stairway to heaven'.

THE BASICS

✚ J8
✉ Place des Ferblantiers
☎ No phone
⏱ Daily 8.30–11.45, 2.30–5.45
🍴 Kosybar (▷ 59)
♿ Moderate (ask for a double ticket that includes entrance to the *minbar*)
❓ Venue for cultural events throughout the year

Tombeaux Saâdiens

HIGHLIGHTS

● Dramatic marble Hall of the Twelve Columns
● The Main Chamber has some fine architectural detail
● Restful garden full of cats

TIPS

● Be prepared to queue. The tombs are found in a small area and it's a popular sight.
● Combine a trip to this royal site with an indulgent visit to La Sultana (▷ 58), Les Bains Marrakech (▷ 58) or Centre Artisanal (▷ 57).

When Moulay Ismail ordered the destruction of any example of the Saâdiens' success, including the Badii Palace (▷ 50–51), he stopped short of disturbing the dead. Instead, he 're-buried' them and then proceeded to wall up the whole site.

Resting place For several hundred years, these great tombs remained untouched and they were not re-discovered until 1917. Princesses and children are buried among the great rulers of the powerful Saâdien dynasty that ruled from 1524 to 1659 and was responsible for Marrakech's Golden Age.

Golden discovery Ahmed El Mansour (known as Ahmed, 'the golden') ordered the construction

Decorative niche at the mausoleum of Ahmed at the Saâdien Tombs (far left); narrow entrance at the tombs (middle left); plaster carving detail (middle right); looking at the highly decorative tiles (middle bottom); El Mansour's tomb in the central chamber (below right)

of the tombs, along with the Badii Palace. Perhaps it is ironic that the Sultan was the first to be buried here in 1603—along with more than 60 of his entourage. Originally the tombs were accessed through the neighbouring mosque, but a special entrance has been created for tourists. Walking through the twisting corridor you can feel as if you are discovering them all over again.

Praise be The first room on the left is the Prayer Hall, followed by the Hall of the Twelve Columns— the largest of the mausoleums, with carved cedar doors, cool Italian marble and an enormous vaulted roof. This is where Ahmed el Mansour and his family are buried. The patterned *zellij* (Moorish mosaic) graves of those not deemed worthy of the mausoleum lie around a peaceful garden with wild roses, hollyhocks and apricot trees.

THE BASICS

✚ H8
✉ Rue de la Kasbah
☎ No phone
🕐 8.30–11.45, 2.30–5.45
🍴 La Sultana de la Medina hotel (▷ 112)
💰 Inexpensive
❓ If you use one of the unpaid on-site guides be sure to tip

More to See

BAB AGNAOU

Its name means 'Gate of the *Gnawa*', after black slaves who were cruelly imported from the neighbouring sub-Saharan countries. Guarding the entrance to the Kasbah, Bab Agnaou was built in the 12th century by the Almohads. One of their masterpieces, it is the most striking gate of the 19 gates in the city walls (▷ 65) with intricate concentric arches and floral details. The elaborate inscriptions from the Koran, bestowing blessings on all who read and enter, are works of art in themselves. Constructed for decoration, rather than defence, Bab Agnaou was certainly at one time even more impressive. It was repeatedly rebuilt and reduced over the years and currently in need of serious restoration.

➕ H8 ✉ Rue de la Kasbah ☎ No phone

CENTRE ARTISANAL

www.bouchaib.net

This centre is like a department store of hand-crafted Moroccan keepsakes. The lower ground floor has smaller items of most interest to visitors; on the upper floors it's mostly furniture and carpets. The big attraction is the fixed prices, but shopping here is not without its frustrations. Not all goods are marked and it can be hard to get (and keep) the attention of sales assistants. They are not always well informed about goods, for example, insisting that an obviously viscose dress is silk. But it's a great one-stop shop and credit cards are accepted. Look out for the lovely, delicately fragranced oils on the ground floor (▷ 57).

➕ H8 ✉ 7 Derb Baissi Kasbah, Boutouil ☎ 024 381 853 🕐 Daily 8.30–7.30

The deocrative stonework of Bab Agnaou only hints at how stunning the gate once was

KASBAH MOSQUE

The green tiled roof and the red walls of the exterior are all that non-Muslims get to see of the mosque. Within the Kasbah walls, between the Agnaou gate (▷ 54) and the Tombeaux Saâdiens (▷ 52–53), it is also known as the El Mansour Mosque after the sultan who built it at the end of the 12th century. Severely damaged in the 16th century, the mosque has been rebuilt and renovated on many occasions.

✚ H8 ✉ Rue de la Kasbah

LANTERN WORKSHOPS

Hidden away from the traffic is this pretty, little square with benches and a simple outdoor café. It is named after the *ferblantiers* (tin workers) whose studios spill out into the square. On sale are handcrafted metal lanterns and mirrors—traditional and modern. Place des Ferblantiers was once called Place de Mellah, and still serves as a point of access to the Jewish quarter, La Mellah (▷ 47).

✚ J8 ✉ Place des Ferblantiers ☎ No phone

PALAIS ROYAL

The royal palace, taking up a huge part of the Kasbah district, is not open to the public, so what goes on behind the towering walls of this complex can only be imagined. Backing on to the mammoth Jardins de l'Agdal (▷ 45), its decorative main entrance stands in contrast with the plain pink walls. King Mohamed VI's newer, much smaller palace is on the other side of the Kasbah but some of the previous king's relatives still live here.

✚ J9 ✉ 8 Rue de la Kasbah ☎ No phone ℹ Not open to the public

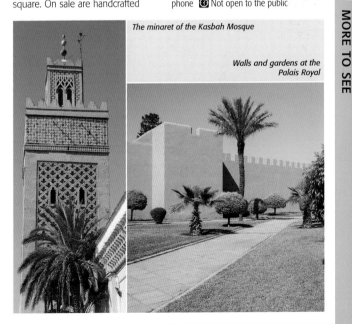

The minaret of the Kasbah Mosque

Walls and gardens at the Palais Royal

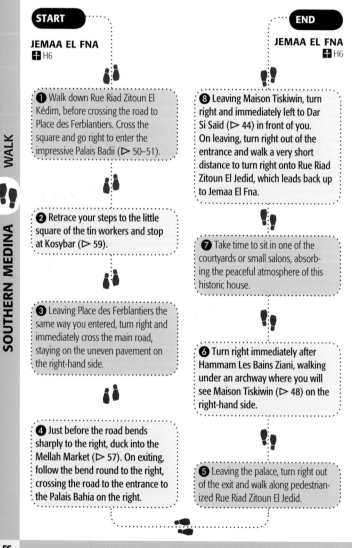

A Royal Tour

Explore the royal quarter of the Kasbah on this leisurely, circular route, visiting two splendid palaces and two interesting museums. Try to do this walk early morning to avoid the heat and crowds.

DISTANCE: 2km (1 mile) **ALLOW:** 4 hours including lunch and visits to sights

START

JEMAA EL FNA
✚ H6

① Walk down Rue Riad Zitoun El Kédim, before crossing the road to Place des Ferblantiers. Cross the square and go right to enter the impressive Palais Badii (▷ 50–51).

② Retrace your steps to the little square of the tin workers and stop at Kosybar (▷ 59).

③ Leaving Place des Ferblantiers the same way you entered, turn right and immediately cross the main road, staying on the uneven pavement on the right-hand side.

④ Just before the road bends sharply to the right, duck into the Mellah Market (▷ 57). On exiting, follow the bend round to the right, crossing the road to the entrance to the Palais Bahia on the right.

END

JEMAA EL FNA
✚ H6

⑧ Leaving Maison Tiskiwin, turn right and immediately left to Dar Si Saïd (▷ 44) in front of you. On leaving, turn right out of the entrance and walk a very short distance to turn right onto Rue Riad Zitoun El Jedid, which leads back up to Jemaa El Fna.

⑦ Take time to sit in one of the courtyards or small salons, absorbing the peaceful atmosphere of this historic house.

⑥ Turn right immediately after Hammam Les Bains Ziani, walking under an archway where you will see Maison Tiskiwin (▷ 48) on the right-hand side.

⑤ Leaving the palace, turn right out of the exit and walk along pedestrianized Rue Riad Zitoun El Jedid.

Shopping

AYAS

www.ayasmarrakech.com

The exquisite silk and cotton clothing for adults and children, along with jewellery, accessories and soft furnishings, have been featured in the pages of style magazines. The shop is next door to the excellent La Tanjia restaurant (▷ 60), so you could conveniently pick up some Moroccan designer items after lunch there.

➕ J8 ✉ 11 Bis Derb Jedid, Rue Bab El Mellah ☎ 024 383 428

CENTRE ARTISANAL

www.bouchaib.net

Hidden away in a corner is the oils section of this artisan centre (▷ 54). Pretty bottles of soothing, sweet smelling orange and rose extract are on sale that can be used to perfume traditional argan oil that is also sold here. Made from the nuts of the rare argan tree (protected by UNESCO), this oil has been credited with dramatic moisturising properties.

➕ H8 ✉ 7 Derb Bâissi Kasbah, Boutouil ☎ 024 381 853

GRAND BIJOUTERIE

The old Jewish jewellery market is a series of arcades with tiny shops shining with gold, silver and coloured gemstones. Pieces are sold by weight so know your price if you want to buy. Most of the

traditional Jewish traders are long gone but it is still an interesting place to see, even if you don't want to buy.

➕ K7 ✉ Rue Bab El Mellah, close to Palais Bahia ☎ No phone 🕐 Daily 9–8

MELLAH MARKET

This fresh food and spice market has been a local institution for half a millennium. If you meet groups of curious tourists on a shopping expedition, chances are they are buying produce for their cookery class kitchen. Come for colour and atmosphere, and to photograph the enormous coloured cones of spices, if not to buy. The squeamish and vegetarians should be warned: The butcher's area (near the entrance from Place des Ferblantiers) is a gory sight, with strung up bloody chickens and fly-covered sheep heads. Live animals abound, too—roosters in crates sit

---

LIVE LIKE ROYALTY

If you want to kit out your place back home in Moroccan royal splendour you could do a lot worse than taking a trip to Centre Artisanal. In just a few hours, and with a budget of less than a couple of thousand dirhams, splendid cushions, lanterns and leather pouffs could all be yours without the need to haggle.

---

among wandering cats. For something altogether more fragrant, head for the multi-coloured roses (the market is just opposite the rose garden) and maybe pick up a big bunch for a few dirhams.

➕ J8 ✉ Between Place des Ferblantiers and Palais Badii ☎ No phone 🕐 Closed Fri am

MOHAMED BOUNMENTEL

Attractive patterned lanterns and containers made out of tin are on sale at this little stall on the square, and at a fraction of the prices charged by boutiques in the new town. Check for scratches and general quality before you buy.

➕ J8 ✉ 12 Place des Ferblantiers ☎ 062 086 010

ORIGINAL DESIGN

Ceramic tableware, as well as vases and ashtrays in an array of bright colours, are on sale here. An assistant can post items around the world if you can't manage purchases in your hand luggage. All the pieces are made by hand—so don't try to bargain as the fixed prices are already very reasonable for such work.

➕ J8 ✉ 47 Place des Ferblantiers, Rue Bab El Mellah ☎ 024 380 361

Entertainment and Activities

GRAND CASINO LA MAMOUNIA

www.grandcasinomamounia.com

Plenty of celebrities have rolled the dice at the large and grand casino attached to the famous hotel. Roulette, black jack and gaming machines are some of the options for gamblers. No jeans, trainers or cameras. Passports required for pay-outs. Admittance to over 16s but gambling for over 18s only.

✚ F7 ✉ 292 Avenue Bad Jedid ☎ 024 444 570 🕐 Daily 3pm–5am

KOSYBAR

A funky spot that is worth a visit any time of day, whether you drink tea from the breezy rooftop terrace, sink into deep sofas on the middle floor, or listen to evening jazz in the ground-floor piano bar. This is the only real bar in this part of the town and many people's favourite watering hole in the medina. It's a relaxing, even romantic spot to indulge in fine wines (some of the best in the country) and excellent, reasonably priced cocktails.

✚ J8 ✉ 47 Place des Ferblantiers ☎ 024 380 324 🕐 Tues–Sun 12–11

LA MAMOUNIA

www.mamounia.com

This grand old hotel is the closest thing the southern medina has to an entertainment centre. Enjoy a cocktail or two in the Churchill piano bar, admire the wonderful gardens and generally soak up a little bit of the decadence this historic establishment has to offer.

✚ F7 ✉ Avenue Bab Jedid ☎ 024 388 600

Spas

LES BAINS DE MARRAKECH

www.lesbainsdemarrakech.com

Squeezed into the Kasbah quarter, this riad spa is fit for a king. If you choose the *gommage* (scrubbing), almost every crevice will be given attention, if the pressure is too much, just say: *'doucement'* (softly). Follow it with a sublime massage before chilling out in the courtyard. Bookings and payment should be made several weeks in advance.

✚ H8 ✉ 2 Derb Sedra, Bab Agnaou, Kasbah ☎ 024 381 428 🕐 Daily 9–8

ANCIENT & MODERN

Although this is the original royal quarter, steeped in tradition and dotted with architectural splendours, there are a few contemporary diversions. Whether you choose betting, drinking, or being massaged, you will find the occasional casino, bar and spa to keep you occupied.

LES BAINS ZIANI

www.hammamziani.ma

Close to the Palais Bahia, this unassuming bathhouse is a good, mid-range option between the expensive, slick spas and the often basic, local hammams (where men wear trunks and women go naked). Jacuzzi, seaweed therapy and massages are all on offer and the service is friendly. This is an experience that will stay with you for a long time. Purchase some of the massage and bath oils—in such delicious fragrances as sweet rose and warm orange—and a scrubbing mitt from reception afterwards to prolong the memory.

✚ J7 ✉ 14 Rue Riad Zitoun El Jedid ☎ 062 715 571 🕐 Daily 7am–10pm

LA SULTANA

www.lasultanamarrakech.com

Perfect for couples, who can be scrubbed down together in a traditional hammam—in large hotels many are segregated. There are a range of packages that could keep you busy for a week. The spa of this smart hotel also has a beauty centre and hairdressers. Bookings are essential as space here is very limited.

✚ H8 ✉ 403 Rue de la Kasbah ☎ 024 388 008 🕐 Daily 8–8

Restaurants

PRICES

Prices are approximate, based on a 3-course meal for one person.

€€€	over €40
€€	€20–€40
€	under €20

KOSYBAR (€€)

One of the few casual spots for a bite to eat in this part of town, it's a good place to visit if you want something light: this relaxed restaurant/bar is known for its sushi and Thai tapas. There are also Moroccan and international options. Choose from Moroccan salads and lightly fried spring rolls as a starter or snack, or more hearty roast lamb or chicken. Desserts tend to have a definite French flavour—sweet soufflés, creamy tarts and caramelized millefeuille. It's open all day, so whether you want a snack or a full meal, there's something to please everyone.

➕ J8 ✉ 47 Place des Ferblantiers ☎ 024 380 324 ⏱ Tue–Sun 12–11

KSAR EL HAMRA (€€)

www.restaurant-ksarelhamra.com

Musicians and oriental dancers entertain diners in this tourist-oriented restaurant serving traditional Moroccan food. Once a riad, there is formal dining in the courtyard or in one of the grand salons.

➕ J7 ✉ 28 Sabt Ben Daoud, Riad Zitoun El Kédim ☎ 024 427 607 ⏱ Most nights, 8pm until early hours

LA MAMOUNIA (€€–€€€)

www.mamounia.com

The buffets at this grand dame of a hotel have long been legendary. There are several, mostly formal, restaurants as well as snack bars, most of which are open to non-residents. There is a dress code (no trainers or shorts) and it is rigorously enforced.

➕ F7 ✉ Avenue Bab Jedid ☎ 024 388 600 ⏱ Daily 3pm–5am

NID CIGOGNE (€–€€)

The snacks, salads and tagines may be mediocre, but this three-storey restaurant has a rooftop terrace with views of nesting storks and is a reasonably priced option right opposite the Saâdien Tombs in the Kasbah

EAT LIKE A KING

To enjoy the best food that this royal quarter has to offer, consider dining at one of the set menu restaurants listed here, all serving traditional Moroccan food. Although not everything may be to your liking, you will be given course after course while serenaded by musicians and even entertained by belly dancers—a night to remember.

district. If you can handle the steep stairs up to the top floor terrace, grab the chance to make the most of the natural air-conditioning and stunning views over the royal quarter.

➕ H8 ✉ 60 Place des Tombeaux Saâdiens ☎ 024 382 092 ⏱ Daily 12–3

PALAIS CALIPAU (€€€)

www.palais-calipau.com

Five-star food from this riad of the same rating. A simple menu (three choices of each) of Moroccan and French cuisine is available first to those staying at the luxury riad, but also to visiting diners who book in advance. This is a chance to enjoy home-cooked cuisine in an intimate setting with a highly personalized service.

➕ J8 ✉ 14 Derb Ben Zina Kasbah ☎ 024 375 583 ⏱ Daily 7pm–11pm

PALAIS GHARNATA (€€€)

www.gharnata.com

In the Jewish Quarter, where places to eat are rather thin on the ground, this sprawling, lavish palace restaurant is frequented by tour groups. An 'evening at the palace' is as much about the surroundings and the musicians and belly dancers as the regulation Moroccan dishes, sometimes served with more formality than attention. The tour groups

often arrive early in the evening, so plan to eat later (after 8.30) if you want to avoid them.

K6 ✉ 5/6 Derb El Arsa ☎ 024 440 615 🕐 Daily 6.30pm–12.30am

LE SABAL (€€)

www.lesabal.com

The decor and atmosphere of this 100-year-old villa is self-assuredly opulent. French and Moroccan food, accompanied by oriental dancers in the large garden when it's warm, or inside by the fire on colder nights. The restaurant prides itself on having hosted intellectuals and artists over the years, but this establishment is old school rather than bohemian.

E5 ✉ Avenue Mohamed V and Place de la Liberté ☎ 024 422 422 🕐 Daily 7pm–1am

LA SULTANA (€€–€€€)

www.lasultanamarrakech.com

Light meals and Mediterranean and Asian-inspired cuisine can be enjoyed by the elegant pool or on the terrace. Dinner means richer French fare in the more formal restaurant. Reservations essential. Vegetarians are catered for here, although don't expect a particularly imaginative choice. The service is generally excellent at this luxury hotel.

H8 ✉ 403 Rue de la Kasbah ☎ 024 388 008 🕐 Daily 12–2, 7.30–9.30

LE TANJIA (€€)

One of a welcome new breed of Marrakechi restaurants that fuse traditional Moroccan food and style with a more contemporary approach. Rocket salads are offered alongside traditional tagines. Knowledgable, relaxed service and a pleasant rooftop terrace. Billed as an Oriental Brasserie, visit during the day for a casual but stylish brunch or lunch. In the evening, tuck into a delicious dinner accompanied by belly dancers and traditional music.

J7 ✉ 14 Derb J'did, Hay Essalam ☎ 024 383 836 🕐 Daily 10am–1am

TATCHIBANA (€€)

www.tatchibana.com

Authentic, Japanese sashimi, melt in the

MEAL WITH A VIEW

Several of the restaurants in this area have rooftop terraces, offering a bird's-eye view of the royal quarter. You might think it's too hot to eat an alfresco lunch but, at most establishments, the tables are shaded by parasols; besides, many of these places get a cool breeze in the afternoon and evening. If you can handle the stairs (most are up three, very steep flights), grab the chance to make the most of their natural air-conditioning and stunning views over the Kasbah.

mouth tempura and barbecued meats, washed down with green tea and international wines. The simple, Zen-like space looking onto a small, walled garden is a breath of fresh air after so many of the over-the-top interiors of many Moroccan restaurants in Marrakech. There is a good value and appealing set menu, which changes with the seasons.

H9 ✉ 38 Derb Bab Ksiba, Kasbah ☎ 024 387 171 🕐 Tue–Sun lunch, dinner

VILLA DES ORANGERS (€€€)

www.villadesorangers.com

The traditional restaurant and bar is elegant if rather formal, and bears the impressive stamp of approval of the esteemed Relais and Châteaux group. Make sure to make reservations as far in advance as possible, as tables are reserved first for in-house guests. The daily changing menu of Mediterranean and Moroccan food is a gastronomic delight—make sure to arrive hungry.

H8 ✉ 6 Rue Sidi Mimoun, Place Ben Tachfine ☎ 024 384 638 🕐 Daily 7pm–11pm

This part of the medina features an important cluster of historic sights. It is dotted with mosques, historic fountains and burgeoning cultural centres. Here are a dense maze of alleyways and the highest concentration of riads in the city—in a quarter known as Mouassine.

Map labels

1

2

Cimetière
Sidi Bel Abbès

Diour Jdad

**Bel Abbès
Sidi Zaouïa**

Ateliers
**Co-operative Artisanale
de Couture Femmes
de Marrakech**

DIOUR JDAD

3

**Zaouïa de
Sidi Ben
Slimane**

D. Arset Ben

D. Sidi Massoud
Ben Brahim

Rue El Cadi

D. Lamsalore

D. Jama

Rue Riad
El Arous

Rue Bab Doukkala

Rue
Bougosr

**Bab
Doukkala**

RUE AHMED OUKOUILA

**BAB
DOUKKALA**

Rue Dar El Bacha

Rue Dar El Bacha

**Mosquée
Sidi Abdelaziz**

D. Sidi Abdelaziz

Rue Mouassine

Rue Diour

4

Rue El Agba

Tribunal

Rue Bab Doukkala

**Bab Doukkala
Mosque**

Rue Fatima
Zohra

Rue Dar El Ghloui

Dar El
Glaoui

**Fontaine de
Mouassine**

**Mosquée
Mouassine**

**Dar
Cherifa**

Rue Sidi El Yamami

5

Bab Er Raha

**Hôtel
de Ville**

**Bab
Nkob**

Avenue Mohamed V

*Cyber Parc Arset
Moulay Abdessalam*

6

0 ___ 200 m

0 ___ 200 yds

E   F   G   H

fechra

Chanem

Bab El
Khêmis

ROUTE DES REMPARTS

Hôpital Chekh
Daoud El Antaki

Rue Bab El Khemis

Collège
Abdel Moumen

Rue El Fakhar

City Walls
and Gates

Bab
Debbagh

Rue Diour et Saboun

Rue de Bab Debbagh

D Soussan

Assouel

Rue

Chrob
ou Chouf
Fountain

Dar
Bellarj

Place du
Moukar

Mosquée
Youssef

Medersa
Ben Youssef

Rue Bin
Lamadene

TANNERIES

moravid
Koubba

Musée de
Marrakech

D Lakdar

J   K   L

Almoravid Koubba

Excavated cistern (middle) and domed interior (right) of Almoravid Koubba (left)

THE BASICS

⊞ J4
✉ Place de la Kissaria
☎ No phone
🕐 Daily 9–1, 2.30–6
💷 Inexpensive

HIGHLIGHTS

● The large Koubba itself, surrounded by deserted gardens and rose bushes
● The ornamental ceiling at the centre, with its fine carvings
● Its key architectural features are the basic elements of Islamic architecture

Also known as Koubba El-Badiyin, this dusty site near the Medersa Ben Youssef is easily overlooked. At first glance, you might think this unprepossessing building is just a waste ground over-run by cats.

Inclusive architecture The Koubba (dome) is worth a look for two reasons: Entrance is included in the reduced 'three-for-one' ticket that includes the Musée de Marrakech (▷ 68–69) and Medersa Ben Youssef (▷ 66–67); and less prosaically, it is the only remaining example of architecture from the Almoravid dynasty, the founders of the city.

Recent discovery Built by Ali Ben Youssef in 1117, the Koubba has existed for close to a millennium but was only uncovered in the 1950s. Watch your step walking down the uneven steps to the original street level where there are some explanation panels in French only.

Ancient bathrooms The Koubba housed an ablutions complex, complete with showers and toilets, for a long-gone mosque, and provided city residents and their livestock with water. The centrepiece is the straw, lime and stone dome with its fine arches and extravagantly decorated ceiling.

Significant inscription The inscription at the entrance reads: *'I was created for science and prayer, by the prince of the believers, descendant of the prophet Abdallah … Pray for him when you enter to fulfil your greatest hopes.'* The words refer both to the founder of the Almoravid dynasty and to the man responsible for this unassuming, but enormously significant building.

TOP 25

City Walls and Gates

If you blot out the traffic chaos and look up to the high fringe of palm trees, it is almost possible to imagine life in the gardens, houses and palaces behind these walls nearly a thousand years ago.

Pretty pink The distinctive pink ramparts encircling the medina separate the old town from the new. Today pedestrians, cars, scooters and *calèches* all funnel through the decorative gates at speed. The ramparts are best appreciated in the early morning or at dusk when the sun gives them a warm, orangey glow.

Impressive structure In 1126, the Almoravid Sultan Ali Ben Youssef began constructing the 10m (33ft) high fortifications to keep out his tribal enemy, the Almohads. The city fell in 1147, but the walls remained, up to 2m (6.5ft) thick in places, with 200 towers and stretching for 16km (10 miles).

Carriage ride A walk around the walls is dusty and noisy. Instead, consider a *calèche* ride in the evening when the traffic has died down. The full circuit takes about an hour and costs around 170 dirhams (€15), but be sure to agree a price first.

Decorative doorways These medieval walls are made of *pisé* (earth) that has proved very durable. The gates that punctuate the medina walls at irregular intervals are all individual—both in form and function. The finely decorated Bab Debbagh and Bab Agnaou (▷ 54) are of spectacular Moorish design. Many gates were added later to increase access to the medina, and these newer ones are much less ornate.

THE BASICS

✚ L4

HIGHLIGHTS

● The view of the walls from a horse drawn carriage (*calèche*) at dusk
● Two of the most notable gates are Bab Debbagh (▷ 70) and Bab Agnaou (▷ 54)
● Imagining the people and traffic that have passed through the gates in nearly 1,000 years

NORTHERN MEDINA ★ **TOP 25**

Medersa Ben Youssef

HIGHLIGHTS

● Peering out of the windows from the first floor gallery
● Reconstructed rooms upstairs
● The serene central courtyard and pool

TIPS

● Information panels are in French only. Bring a mini dictionary or consider hiring a local guide.
● It can be difficult to find the school on your own, even using a map; ask a local if necessary.

This Koranic boarding school is one of the few religious sites non-Muslims can enter. There is real serenity in the architecture, so—more than anywhere else in Marrakech—time your visit to avoid tour groups.

School of thought One of the largest centres for religious education in North Africa, Ben Youssef was founded in the 14th century. Re-built by the Saâdiens around 1570, it has not been used as a school since 1960.

Light and shade The entrance is through a rather dark corridor that opens onto a beautiful, sunlit colonnaded courtyard, bathed in sunlight and dominated by a large, rectangular pool. Influenced by Andalusian architecture, around it are multi-coloured *zellij* (Moorish mosaic) tiling and intricate

Entrance onto the central courtyard at Ben Youssef Medersa (left); school sign (middle top); tiled column detail (middle bottom); stucco and cedar carving (top right); pine cone and leaf detail in the Prayer Hall (bottom right)

stucco panels. Behind the pool is the domed Prayer Hall, full of intricately carved cedar, stylized palm motifs and inscriptions from the Koran.

Cramped quarters Two staircases from the entrance lead up to over 100 tiny student rooms that were once occupied by 900 students. Avoid the swarms of photographing and posing tourists who dart in and out of the honeycomb of cells. Find an empty one, shut the door and imagine what it was like to be one of the students.

Living history Two of the rooms have been reconstructed to contain all the basic things a student would have—a mat for sleeping on, a tea set and a writing desk. Kate Winslet got to know this *medersa* (theological college) when it was transformed into the school of an Algerian Sufi mystic in her 1998 film, *Hideous Kinky*.

THE BASICS

➕ J4
✉ Off Souk el Khemis
☎ 024 390 911
🕐 Apr–end Sep Sat–Thu 9–7; Oct–end Mar Sat–Thu 9-6
🍴 Café next door in Musée de Marrakech
♿ Expensive; combination ticket can be purchased, which includes entrance to Musée de Marrakech and Almoravid Koubba

Musée de Marrakech

TOP
25

The beautiful tiled and patterned Musée de Marrakech contains some fine objects

➕ J4

✉ Place Ben Youssef

☎ 024 441 893

🕐 9.30–7

🍴 Pleasant courtyard café

💰 Expensive; combination ticket can be purchased to include entrance to Medersa Ben Youssef and Almoravid Koubba

❓ Guided tours available. One of the very few air-conditioned buildings in the old city.
There is limited information regarding the exhibition and that is only in French

HIGHLIGHTS

● The hammam, filled with a huge white sofa, is a delight
● The still functioning toilets
● Listening to the music while sitting in the central courtyard

This late-19th century palace is an elegant expression of classical Andalusian architecture. The star exhibit of this museum is the building itself, with its fine central courtyard and former palace hammam now used as an exhibition space.

Sound of music In the centre of the cool, serene main courtyard is an impressive fountain and chandelier, surrounded by comfortable chairs—a lovely, relaxing spot. Traditional music (CDs of which can be bought in the museum shop) adds to the atmosphere.

Islamic arts The salons and archways off the main courtyard contain interesting permanent exhibitions with the emphasis on traditional Islamic arts. Examples of Arabic calligraphy and age-old Korans are here, along with Islamic coins dating back to the 8th century and traditional costumes from Fez and the Atlas Mountains.

Mountain pieces Linger over the delicate Berber embroidery, textiles and jewellery, including some notable silver hands of Fatima—a good luck charm—as well as powerful old black and white photos of women from the Atlas Mountains. Towards the rear, the ceramics section with highly decorated pottery is not to be missed; not least for the finely worked ceiling.

Art and function In the former kitchens the changing exhibitions of contemporary art are of varying quality, but some significant Moroccan artists are represented. Even the toilet—with its traditional tiling and brass taps—is a work of art.

Tanneries

HIGHLIGHTS

● Catching a glimpse of a
vanishing trade
● The enormous vats of
colourful dyes—like a giant
paint box

TIPS

● Accept the offer of a sprig
of mint (or bring your own
nosegay) to hide the stench.
● Bring your own guide if
you would rather not go it
alone. Your riad or hotel
can suggest a guide to
accompany you.

**The highly skilled craftsmen who work
in the tanneries live, quite literally, on
the edge of society. Carrying out a trade
that has been passed down through
generations from medieval times
until today, they have now gained an
international reputation.**

Water's edge The city's tanneries are perched
right on the edge of the medina, not to isolate the
terrible stench but for easy access to water from
the Oued Issil stream that runs beyond the decorated Bab Debbagh, or tanners' gate. This is the
sight where you will be bothered most by would-
be 'guides', partly because the tanneries are quite
difficult to find, but also because they want a fee
for handing out mint (against the foul smell) and
to show you around.

Preparing the skins (top left); dying vats at the Rue de Bab Debbagh (bottom far left); skins waiting to be dyed (bottom left); a view of the tannery and vats (middle); a boquet of mint smells better than the tannery (top right); the end product—babouches, Moroccan traditional slippers (bottom right)

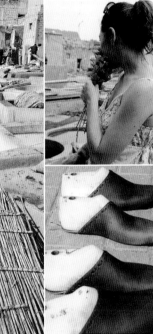

Animal treatment In a 20-day process virtually unchanged since medieval times, cow, goat, sheep and camel skins are stripped (the squeamish should steer clear). The skins are then placed in a vat of water and blood, which strengthens them.

Colourful process After the vat, the skins are dunked into animal urine and pigeon droppings to soften them. Tanners can be seen working in hell-ish conditions, waist deep in vats of natural dyes such as saffron for yellow, indigo for blue and poppies for red. Finally, the skins are dried in the sun before being made into handbags, lamps and *babouches* (Moroccan slippers).

Hell on earth These working conditions have spawned all kinds of legends, in which tanners are seen as demons condemned to a hellish life.

THE BASICS

- K4
- Rue de Bab Debbagh, Tanners District
- No phone
- Daily 9.30–6
- Inexpensive

More to See

BAB DOUKKALA MOSQUE

The soaring minaret of this mosque makes it a local landmark although as with all mosques in Marrakech, non-Muslims are not allowed to enter. Built in the 16th century, with the Sidi El Hassan fountain outside, it continues to serve this thriving quarter of the medina. Rue Bab Doukkala, which runs from the former palace of Dar El Bacha (closed to visitors) through the gate of the same name was once the old road to the Berber region of Doukkala. The ornate gate still stands, but traffic now passes through an adjacent modern gate.

🞦 G4 ⊠ Rue Bab Doukkala ☎ No phone

BEL ABBÈS SIDI ZAOUÏA

Non-Muslims can catch a glimpse of the large, open courtyard and some of the buildings of this religious complex, but are not allowed to enter. Twelfth-century Bel Abbès Sidi was the most celebrated of seven saints whose tombs have formed part of a popular pilgrimage since the 17th century. Bel Abbès was said to give sight to the blind, and even today the blind and disabled are looked after here. His tomb is in a nearby cemetery. Open for worship but not visitors.

🞦 H2 ⊠ Rue Sidi Ghanem

CHROB OU CHOUF FOUNTAIN

The name of this ornate public fountain translates as 'Drink and Admire', after one of its inviting Arabic inscriptions. It was built on the orders of Sultan Ahmad al-Mansour (1578-1603), the most powerful of all Saâdien rulers. Providing water for his people had spiritual as well as practical meaning because of the Koranic importance of cleanliness. It also showed him to be a man of charity, taste and learning. The fountain is in a tall recess below a wooden arch covered in beautiful engravings and carvings.

🞦 J4 ⊠ Just off Rue Bab Taghzout ☎ No phone 🖑 Free

Bab Doukkala Mosque

Courtyard and buildings at Bel Abbès Sidi Zaouïa

COOPERATIVE ARTISANALE DE COUTURE FEMMES DE MARRAKECH

This cooperative supports some of the poorest women in the city, providing them with fair wages and working conditions. As well as selling fashions and fabrics from their shop, they supply fair trade outlets in Europe.
🔀 K3 ✉ 2 Derb El Akkari (1st floor), Bin Lamaassir ☎ 024 378 308

DAR BELLARJ

The 'Stork's Head' cultural centre is just north of Medersa Ben Youssef, before the mosque of the same name. This is a low-key venue of interest as a skilfully restored historical building as much as for its artistic happenings. The building used to be a hospital for storks, which are held sacred in Marrakech. The centre opened in 1999, with the courtyard and centrepiece fountain painstakingly restored. However, it is only really worth a special visit and the entrance fee if there happens to be an event or exhibition. Check for details in the local press and look out for theatrical performances and workshops, too.
🔀 J4 ✉ 9 Rue Toulat Zaouiat Lahdar ☎ 024 444 555 👆 Moderate

DAR CHERIFA

www.marrakech-riads.net
Hidden deep in the souks, this literary café in a beautifully restored townhouse puts on temporary, and often informal, art exhibitions. The work of Moroccan and international artists is displayed in this simple, but attractive place. There are also casual musical performances and occasional cultural events. It's a relaxing spot for a juice or even lunch in the courtyard, and for the books on Moroccan art and culture in the tiny library. Dar Cherifa was a pioneer in the movement to bring European art and cultural centres to the heart of Marrakech.
🔀 H5 ✉ 8 Derb Charfa Lakbir Mouassine, off Rue Sidi El Yamani ☎ 024 426 463

Brass sign at Dar Bellarj

Shopping

BAB DOUKKALA

This daily food market is a wonderful, colourful place to wander whether you want to buy or not. Among wheelbarrows full of fresh mint, bloody sheep heads and piles of glossy purple aubergines, locals carefully scrutinize the offerings and share a joke as they bargain with the sellers. The market is open daily from 8am until 7pm, except on Fridays when it is open 9am until noon.

➕ G4 ✉ Rue Bab Doukkala ☎ No phone

KIFKIF

www.kifkifbystef.com
Morocco with a funky twist, using bright colours, pretty fabrics, delicate tailoring and fine embroidery; also more traditional raffia shoes and leather bags. Pieces are made with international tourists in mind and you will find prices in euros.

➕ H5 ✉ 8 Rue El Ksour, Bab El Ksour ☎ 061 082 041

KULCHI

Whether you are after a pop art T-shirt from a Moroccan designer, some exotic East African textiles, or something colourful from owner Florence Taranne's own label, you should find it here. She also has a small boutique in the Comptoir (▷ 92) restaurant, and sells trendy lounge music CDs.

➕ H5 ✉ 1 Rue El Ksour, Bab El Ksour ☎ No phone

MUSTAPHA BLAOUI

An unprepossessing entrance opens into a large interior, stacked high with affordable ceramics, lanterns and pouffes, as well as high-priced furniture and antiques. Don't miss it.

➕ G5 ✉ 142–144 Rue Bab Doukkala ☎ 024 385 240

LA PORTE D'OR

Prices in the 'Golden Door' aren't cheap; you'll find hand-carved doors along with finely worked, colourful Berber rugs and individual antique finds.

➕ J5 ✉ 115 Souk Semmarine ☎ 024 445 454

LA QOUBBA

www.art-gallery-marrakech.com
Moroccan and international art is for sale in

SOUKS GALORE

There are shopping opportunities galore to be had in the seemingly never-ending souks, and even 'shopaphobics' will find it difficult to ignore the insistent pleas of the shop keepers in this area. It is hard to escape this huge market place, but there really is something for everyone. As well as listing some of the more interesting souks (areas full of competing specialist shops), we have focussed on some individual and recognizable shops, where you will have a memorable experience and find that special item.

this long-standing art gallery near the Marrakech Museum, with regularly changing and permanent exhibitions.

➕ J4 ✉ 91 Souk Talaa ☎ 024 380 515

SOUK DES BABOUCHES

This souk sells—yes you've guessed it— babouches, those traditional Moroccan slippers. Pick from a rainbow spectrum of colours and bear in mind that not all of these shoes are leather —some are plastic.

➕ J5 ☎ No phone

SOUK DES TAPIS

The carpet souk is draped with rugs for your floors, or even your walls. Take your time before committing to such a big purchase; there are a number of shops stuffed with carpets made in Marrakech, the mountains and even further afield.

➕ J5 ☎ No phone

SOUK DES TEINTURIERS

Draped with bright blue, orange and red wools, the Dyer's Souk is the most photogenic of them all. The little stalls, however, tend to specialize in metalwork, lanterns and ceramics, rather than woollen goods.

➕ J5 ☎ No phone

Cookery Courses

LA MAISON ARABE

www.lamaisonarabe.com
Cooking workshops take place in the lovely gardens of this villa—a 20-minute taxi journey from the medina. Like most cookery courses, the emphasis is on enjoyment and participants get to eat their creations for lunch. Small groups and plenty of inspiration, as well as advice about where to buy spices and tagines in the town. You can also dine in the villa's restaurant (▷ 76), to discover how it really should taste.
➕ G5 ✉ 1 Derb Assehbe ☎ 024 387 010

RIAD ENIJA

www.riadenija.com
One-day cookery courses tailored to individual needs—whether you want to know how to make your couscous fluffy, or the best way to choose spices. After a visit to the local spice market enjoy a private cooking lesson in the riad kitchen. The Riad Enija cookbook is a beautifully photographed delight, with inspiring menus to try at home. All budding Jamie Olivers should give it a try.
➕ J5 ✉ Riad Enija, Place Rabba Kédim, 9 Derb Mesfioui ☎ 024 440 926

Cultural Centres and Galleries

DAR BELLARJ
(▷ 72)

DAR CHERIFA
(▷ 72)

MINISTERO DEL GUSTO

www.ministerodelgusto.com
'The Ministry of Taste' is an eclectic, unashamedly post-modern gallery that embraces a wide range of contemporary design. When you visit (appointments preferred) it might be showing one-off furniture pieces, or a collection of vintage fashion. Commissions for furniture design are taken here, and a wide variety of desirable *objets d'art* for the home are on sale.
➕ H5 ✉ Derb Azouz 22, Mouassine ☎ 024 426 455

MAKE A MEAL OF IT

There are very few places in this part of town to enjoy an alcoholic drink. Make the most of your riad (if it has a drinks licence) with a pre-dinner cocktail on the rooftop, or a nightcap afterwards. Most of the restaurants in town (but few of the pavement cafés around Jemaa El Fna) have a drinks licence—just don't expect to stumble across a bar in the medina.

MOULAY ABDESLAM CYBER PARK

www.arsatmoulayabdeslam.ma
Most Marrakechis and visitors come here to escape the traffic-clogged streets of the 21st-century city and to relax by one of the fountains or in the shade of an orange tree. This royal park filled with ancient palm trees has been transformed into a 'cyber park', sponsored by high-tech companies such as Philips and Microsoft. It is an 8ha (20-acre) Wi-Fi zone (although few laptops can be seen) dotted with rather ugly, and not always functioning, Internet terminals.
➕ F6 ✉ Avenue Mohamed V, (entrance opposite Ensemble Artisanal) ☎ No telephone 🕐 Daily 9am–7pm 🎫 Free

Nightlife

AL'ANBAR

www.alanbar-marrakech.com
Lounge, bar, disco, restaurant and belly dancers. What more could you need? One of the few places in the northern medina (other than riads) to get an alcoholic drink. Live DJs on weekends and some weekdays add volume.
➕ G5 ✉ Rue Jbel Lakhdar ☎ 044 380 763

NORTHERN MEDINA

ENTERTAINMENT AND ACTIVITIES

Restaurants

PRICES

Prices are approximate, based on a 3-course meal for one person.

€€€ over €40
€€ €20–€40
€ under €20

CAFÉ BOURGANVILLEA (€–€€)

This riad-restaurant offers really good international and Moroccan food, as well as tea and *petits fours*. Sit in the courtyard, shady terrace or in one of the comfortable lounges.
✚ H4 ✉ 33 Rue Mouassine ☎ 024 441 111 🕐 Tues–Sun 10am–9pm

LA FOUNDOUK (€€€)

www.foundouk.com
An old favourite serving consistently good food, although in a rather gloomy setting. Come for a light lunch of salmon quiche and pistachio sorbet. Evening options are richer—French dishes, traditional Moroccan fare and even Thai chicken.
✚ J4 ✉ 55 Souk Hal Fassi, Kat Bennahïs ☎ 024378 190 🕐 Tue–Sun 12–12

LA MAISON ARABE (€€)

www.lamaisonarabe.com
This riad restaurant opened in the 1940s and is one of the city's oldest. Still retaining its colonial air, the two international and Moroccan restaurants can feel rather stuffy. Visit instead for cocktails and

Asian-inspired tapas or take tea in the courtyard,
✚ G4 ✉ 1 Derb Assehbe ☎ 024 387 010 🕐 Daily 8am–midnight

LE PAVILION (€€€)

Excellent French food is served in this intimate, yet formal restaurant either in cozy alcoves or in the courtyard under a huge tree. It's quite difficult to find, so ask in your riad for clear directions.
✚ G4 ✉ 47 Derb Zaouia, Rue Bab Doukkala ☎ 024 387 040 🕐 Daily 7pm–12

LE TOBSIL (€€€)

A candidate for the city's best restaurant, the set meal is accompanied by musicians and includes aperitifs and drinks. Tables in both the courtyard and gallery can be a little too close together for comfort. Reservations are essential.
✚ G6 ✉ 22 Derb Abdellah ben Hessaien, R'mila Bab Ksour ☎ 024 441 523 🕐 Wed–Mon 8pm–11.30pm

RIAD RESTAURANTS

The Northern Medina contains the highest concentration of riads in Marrakech. Most of them offer home-cooked meals to their guests but also to non-residents. Don't miss the chance to dine at your riad, but consider the chance to eat at one of the other numerous riads in this area. Just remember to reserve ahead.

YACOUT (€€€)

A local institution and very firmly on the map of Marrakechi restaurants, although not quite the star of the scene it used to be. Begin with an aperitif on the terrace before tucking into a three-course Moroccan feast. Reservations essential.
✚ G3 ✉ 79 Derb Sidi Ahmed Soussi, Rue Bab Doukkala ☎ 024 382 900 🕐 Tue–Sun 7pm–late

Cafés

CAFÉ DES ÉPICES (€–€€)

www.cafedesepices.net
This lovely, friendly little spot is a rare place to relax in the mayhem of the souks. Three floors overlook a square filled with spice and straw-hat sellers. Enjoy a mint tea, simple salads or sandwiches and take in the changing wall art.
✚ J5 ✉ 75 Place Rabba Kédim ☎ 024 391 770 🕐 Daily 10am–11pm

TERRASSE DES ÉPICES (€–€€)

www.terrassedesepices.com
Sister restaurant of the Café des Épices offering salads, brochettes and chocolate desserts, as well as cultural and art evenings. Simple, yet elegant decor; chocolate coloured rooms and a rooftop terrace with wonderful views.
✚ H4 ✉ 15 Souk Cherifia, Sidi Abdelaziz ☎ 024 375 904 🕐 Daily 9am–11pm

European-style entertainment and relaxation with a Moroccan twist are just a stone's throw from the medieval medina. Marrakech's two most notable gardens are here, along with a lovely little collection of chic boutiques and restaurants that wouldn't be out of place in Paris or Rome.

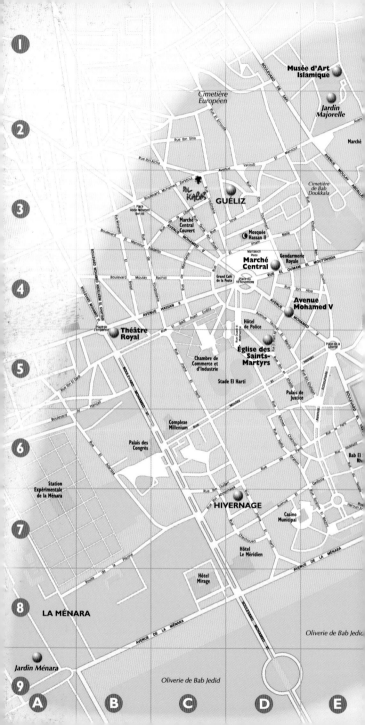

I

2

3

4

5

6

7

8

9

A **B** **C** **D** **E**

Cimetière
Européen

Rue El Ermnatia

Rue Ibn Sina

Rue Ibn Aïcha

Boulevard Mohamed

AL KABRS

GUÉLIZ

Place Abdel Moumen
ben Ali

Marché
Central
Couvert

AVENUE MOHAMED

Mosquée
Nassan II

Imam

Vacoub

Avenue

Mansoar

Mansour

Siraa

Malik

Marrakech
Plaza

**Marché
Central**

Gendarmerie
Royale

RUE EL OUMAM

RUE EL MOUTTAHIDA

Boulevard

Boulevard

Mansour

Fdalsity

Boulevard Moulay Rachid

BOULEVARD MOHAMED ABDELKRIM EL KHATTABI

BOULEVARD MOHAMED

Youssouara

Grand Café
de la Poste

AVENUE HASSAN II

Place du
16 Novembre

Ibn Atra

AVENUE

**Avenue
Mohamed V**

MOHAMED

Place de
la Liberté

Rue

Qadi

Ayad

Guéliz

Rue El Imam Malik

**Théâtre
Royal**

Place de
l'Empereur

Chambre de
Commerce et
d'Industrie

Rue Oued El Makhazine

Hôtel
de Police

**Église des
Saints-
Martyrs**

BOULEVARD MOHAMED V

Stade El Harti

Rue El Harti

Moulay

Palais de
Justice

BOULEVARD EL YAI

Rue de Paris

Complexe
Millenium

**Bab El
Rh**

Palais des
Congrès

Rue

Rue Ibn Oudaï

Station
Expérimentale
de la Ménara

Boulevard

Al Mansour

Rue El Andalous

HIVERNAGE

Avenue

Casino
Municipal

Harout Er

Piscine

Avenue de la Menara

Chrichtouen

Hôtel
Le Méridien

Avenue

Mohamed VI

LA MÉNARA

AVENUE DE LA MÉNARA

Hôtel
Mirage

AVENUE DE LA MÉNARA

Oliverie de Bab Jedic

Boulevard

Jardin Ménara

Oliverie de Bab Jedid

**Musée d'Art
Islamique**

**Jardin
Majorelle**

Marché

AVENUE MOULAY ABDELI

Cimetière
de Bab
Doukkala

BOULEVARD DE SAFI

RUE DE FÈS
La Palmeraie
Cimetière

AVENUE DU 11 JANVIER

*Cimetière
Sidi Ahmed
Es Zaw'ia*

AVENUE

ALLAL

FASSI

JACQUES

Mansour

AVENUE DU 11 JANVIER

GARE
ROUTIÈRE

Bâb
ukkala

BOULEVARD EL YARMOUK

0   200 m
0   200 yds

F   G   H   J

Guéliz

HIGHLIGHTS

● Eating, drinking and shopping in the charming boutiques and brasseries
● Sampling the European side of the city

TIPS

● Don't visit on a Sunday when most of the shops are closed. Do bear in mind, however, that many close for lunch until 3.30pm and stay open until 7pm.
● Although Guéliz is not far from the medina, it's a dusty, noisy walk. Take a taxi or calèche instead.

The highlights of this neighbourhood are clustered together and best explored on foot (▷ 89), visiting lovely little shops and grazing at atmospheric cafés and restaurants. Here, you will see the boldest examples of old Marrakech reinvented.

European indulgence European-style entertainment and relaxation with a Moroccan twist are still very close to the medieval medina. Marrakech's most notable garden is here, along with a charming collection of chic boutiques and restaurants that wouldn't be out of place in many major European cities.

Newer than new The French built the *Ville Nouvelle* (New Town) with its wide, leafy Parisian-style avenues between 1912 and 1956. The New City strictly speaking is made up of Guéliz and Hivernage, but today the real New City is found in La Palmeraie.

Items for sale in Guéliz—bracelets from Michele Baconnier in Rue de Vieux (top far left); tea glasses from L'Orientaliste in Rue de la Liberté (top right); colourful Frederique Birkemeyer dresses at Intensité Nomade in rue de la Liberte (bottom left); plenty of choice for souvenirs at L'Orientaliste (below)

Fashion Marrakech In the New City, young designers sell jazzed-up camouflage *jellabahs* (traditional kaftans) and exquisite, contemporary takes on artisan jewellery. Leather from the tanneries is crafted into fashionable bags and the city's traditional lanterns have been updated for the 21st century.

THE BASICS

➕ D3

Hedonistic attractions Guéliz has very few historic or important sights as such, but its light, bright European-style shops and eateries are the perfect antidote to the dizzying depths of the exotic medieval medina.

Resting place The Cimetiere Européen (European Cemetery) on Rue Erraouda, the burial place of colonists and their children provides a more sombre note. This walled burial ground dotted with mausoleums contains a white obelisk dedicated to soldiers killed in World War II and is a peaceful, well-kept spot.

Jardin Majorelle

HIGHLIGHTS

● The Musée d'Art Islamique
(▷ 86)
● The pretty Monet-like
lily pond
● Pausing on one of the
peaceful benches to survey
the scene

TIPS

● Don't forget to visit the
boutique for some unusual
souvenirs.
● Take a *calèche* or taxi
from the medina.

**French artist Jacques Majorelle (1886–
1962) produced restrained, obscure
watercolours, while his father Louis made
furniture. Yet their most impressive work
was this joint effort outside both their
specialist fields.**

Pretty and painterly This cool blue oasis in the
pink desert city is both a finely designed botanic
garden and relaxing retreat, with soaring palms and
painterly detail. Plants of the five continents are
exposed in a enchanting framework. Opened in
1947, the gardens were coloured with the revolu-
tionary bright hue that became known as *Majorelle
bleu*. When Jacques died, the garden fell into disre-
pair before being bought by Marrakech resident and
fashion designer Yves Saint Laurent in 1980.

Clockwise from far left: garden gateway at Jardin Majorelle; pathway through the bamboo forest; the Museum of Islamic Arts overlooks a pretty lily pond; flowering cactus; family outing to the Jardin Majorelle

Green retreat A trickling fountain at the entrance gives way to a rustling bamboo forest. To the right is the garden's most memorable view through to a lily pond reminiscent of Monet. The global collection of plants includes cacti and banana trees under which visitors sit on benches to read, to snooze or to kiss. The garden is dotted with blue terracotta pots, wandering turtles and 15 species of birds, some of them rare.

Heaven on earth Jardin Majorelle follows the design rules of all Islamic gardens, as laid out in the Koran. Enclosed by walls, with water at its heart, it boasts lush vegetation and simple architecture. Although intended to be a serene earthly paradise, this small garden often becomes overrun with visitors, so try to visit first thing in the morning.

THE BASICS

www.jardinmajorelle.com

➕ E2

✉ Avenue Yacoub El Mansour, Guéliz

☎ 024 301 852

🕐 Jun–end Sep daily 8–6; Oct–end May daily 8–5

🍴 Lovely courtyard café serves delicious juices, snacks and sandwiches (▷ 93)

💰 Expensive; separate museum entrance moderate

Jardin Ménara

HIGHLIGHTS

● Views of the Atlas Mountains from the upper pavilion
● Luxuriating in this historic and romantic setting

TIPS

● There is a small charge to enter the pavilion, which is well worth it.
● Don't expect a traditional European garden.
● The ideal time to visit is during the late afternoon.

Ménara derives from *minzah*, meaning pavilion, and also 'beautiful view'. The world's grandest reservoir is the centrepiece of the Ménara garden, like a swimming lake for the ancient gods, with its fine pavilion and spectacular mountain backdrop.

Stuff of legends The view is best in winter and spring, when the pavilion is framed by the snow-capped Atlas Mountains (between May and September a heat haze obscures the peaks). Legend has it that sultans would entertain their lovers in this romantic setting. One particularly petulant sultan had a habit of casting guests into the waters, but today only fish disturb the peace, leaping to catch the insects, and it's the perfect place to escape the hustle and bustle of the city.

Strolling in the Jardin Ménara (top far left); a view across the gardens from the minzah (top left); a view of the minzah and the basin with a mountain backdrop (bottom left); enjoying a camel ride (middle); irrigation drain by the palms (top right); walking through the olives (bottom right)

Royal retreat The present pavilion was built in the 19th century replacing one erected some 300 years earlier. But these were just royal ornaments around a purpose-built oasis enabling crops to grow.

Desert watering hole The lake was constructed in the 12th century when most of North Africa was ruled from Marrakech. Underground channels called *khettaras* brought water from the mountains 30km (19 miles) away. This is no ornamental garden, and there is not a flowerbed in sight. Instead, olive groves surround and you can see olives being harvested between October and January.

Pavilion attraction In the Ménara pavilion take in the view from the upper level. Just before dusk, when the day has cooled and the crowds have gone, the sunset adds to the romance.

THE BASICS

+ A9
- Avenue de la Ménara, Hivernage
- No phone
- Daily 8.30–6
- Down some steps from the lake there is a pleasant café for light refreshments
- Garden free; pavilion entry inexpensive
- Sound and Light Show is only recommended if you like waving banners and old-fashioned dancing

Musée d'Art Islamique

Striking objects from the Musée d'Art Islamique

The intimate Museum of Islamic Art in is Jacques Majorelle's old painting studio. It now contains Yves Saint-Laurent's personal collection, including Berber jewellery and weapons, as well as some Majorelle paintings.

Attractive collection Although part of the Jardin Majorelle, a separate entrance fee is payable to enter the museum. Indeed, it is a separate attraction altogether. A modern addition to the garden that is often overlooked, this museum is a not-to-be missed personal collection of Islamic art.

Inspired The workshop was, of course, a place of imagination and of inspiration, a kind of fairy tale house in the middle of this seen-to-be-believed garden. Yves Saint-Laurent was famously inspired by the city, his work resonating with its patterns and colours. Its present-day purpose is perhaps more serious and a tribute to the Islamic culture that inspired both the great artist and the world-renowned designer. What better way to exemplify the fusion of the flamboyant fashion tastes of the French and the serious, detailed work of the Islamists?

Cultural appreciation Like Maison Tiskiwin (▷ 48), this is an example of a highly personal collection in a very special building. With little or no pretension, it shows a heartfelt appreciation of the local culture. Just four small rooms contain exhibits such as antique Berber jewellery, carved wooden doors, delicate embroidery, textiles and medieval manuscripts, as well as lithographs and pieces of art by Majorelle that relate to the area.

THE BASICS

www.jardinmajorelle.com
⊕ E1
✉ Avenue Yacoub el Mansour, Guéliz
☎ 024 301 852
🕐 Jun–end Sep daily 8–6; Oct–end May daily 8–5
🍴 Lovely courtyard café onsite serves delicious juices, snacks and sandwiches within the gardens (▷ 93)
💰 Expensive; separate museum entrance moderate

HIGHLIGHTS

● Islamic art collection often overlooked by tourists
● Explanations in English and air-conditioning makes viewing a pleasure
● Antique Berber items

More to See

AVENUE MOHAMED V

Mohamed V, grandfather of the current ruler, negotiated independence from France in 1956. A national hero in Morocco, the main thoroughfare in most Moroccan cities is named after him. In Marrakech, it is punctuated by the two huge roundabouts of Place de la Liberté and Place du 16 Novembre, where it intersects with Avenue Hassan II, named after Mohamed VI's father. Parallel to the west is Avenue Mohamed VI, symbolically renamed from Avenue de France.

🚹 D4

ÉGLISE DES SAINTS-MARTYRS

The Catholic Church of the Holy Martyrs lies just off Avenue Mohamed V. One of the first buildings in the New City, it still continues to serve a small church-going population. It is thought that the name Guéliz comes from a corruption of '*église*', which for the Arab population characterized the French. Its rather plain exterior and simple tower pales into comparison with the splendid, towering minarets of mosques throughout this largely Muslim city.

🚹 D5 ✉ Rue El Imam Ali, Guéliz
☎ 024 430 585

MARCHE CENTRAL

The covered Central Market on Avenue Mohamed V, northwest of Place du 16 November, was once the corner stone of local life. The animated street market that sold food, flowers and even alcohol had been an important meeting place and landmark since it was constructed in the 1920s. In an almost unfathomable move, it was razed to the ground in 2005 to make way for the Eden development, a multi-million dollar shopping mall with luxury apartments and underground parking. The markets demise drew fierce opposition but it was considered essential for the 'evolution' of the city.

🚹 D4 ✉ Avenue Mohamed V

The simple exterior of the Église des Saints Martyrs reveals a cool, plain but attractive interior

HIVERNAGE

This exclusive residential area west of the medina is known mostly for its sprawling villas and five-star, international chain hotels. While this was once the area for upmarket hotels and entertainment, the focus has very definitely moved to La Palmeraie. Most visitors come at night to eat and be entertained at Le Comptoir Darna (▷ 92), perhaps passing the defunct Palais des Congrès on the way to the Jardin Ménara (▷ 84–85).

➕ D7

LA PALMERAIE

Named after its 12th-century date palm plantation, La Palmeraie flourished in the desert thanks to a sophisticated irrigation system. Nowadays, it is a patchwork of luxury rural resorts and dusty building sites —not an area for sightseeing. Dubbed the Beverley Hills of Morocco, swish hotels and extravagant villas attract a wealthy Moroccan and international set. The rest of us come to play a few holes at one of the multiplying golf courses or, in the evening, dress up for the extravagant restaurants and European-style nightclubs.

➕ J1

THÉÂTRE ROYAL

Respected Moroccan architect, Charles Boccara designed the Royal Theatre, with its splendid portico and dome. Inaugurated in 2001, the theatre is a key venue for the annual Popular Arts Festival in July, when there are nightly musical and theatrical performances. It also hosts the Moroccan Philharmonic Orchestra. The pièce de résistance is the 1,200-seat open-air amphitheatre, adding extra drama to opera and dance performances. Shows and exhibitions are held throughout the year—information is available from the tourist ofice.

➕ B5 ✉ 40 Avenue Mohamed VI, Guéliz ☎ 024 431 516

Camel rides at La Palmeraie (top);
Fountain at Hivernage (above);
Courtyard interior at the Théâtre Royal (right)

Guéliz

This easy-to-follow little circuit is a hedonistic shopping spree, punctuated by some of the city's most charming cafés. Most of the boutiques here are closed for lunch from around 1pm until 3.30pm, as well as on Sundays.

DISTANCE: 1.5km (1 mile)   **ALLOW:** 2 hours

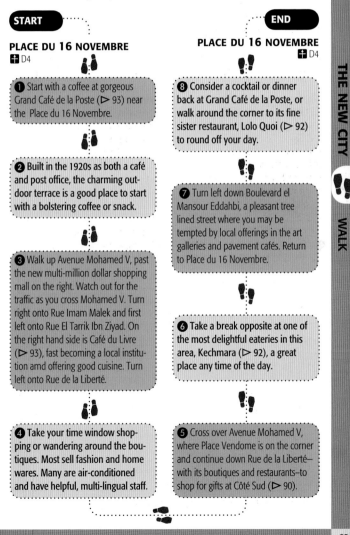

START

PLACE DU 16 NOVEMBRE
🚩 D4

① Start with a coffee at gorgeous Grand Café de la Poste (▷ 93) near the Place du 16 Novembre.

② Built in the 1920s as both a café and post office, the charming outdoor terrace is a good place to start with a bolstering coffee or snack.

③ Walk up Avenue Mohamed V, past the new multi-million dollar shopping mall on the right. Watch out for the traffic as you cross Mohamed V. Turn right onto Rue Imam Malek and first left onto Rue El Tarrik Ibn Ziyad. On the right hand side is Café du Livre (▷ 93), fast becoming a local institution amd offering good cuisine. Turn left onto Rue de la Liberté.

④ Take your time window shopping or wandering around the boutiques. Most sell fashion and home wares. Many are air-conditioned and have helpful, multi-lingual staff.

END

PLACE DU 16 NOVEMBRE
🚩 D4

⑧ Consider a cocktail or dinner back at Grand Café de la Poste, or walk around the corner to its fine sister restaurant, Lolo Quoi (▷ 92) to round off your day.

⑦ Turn left down Boulevard el Mansour Eddahbi, a pleasant tree lined street where you may be tempted by local offerings in the art galleries and pavement cafés. Return to Place du 16 Novembre.

⑥ Take a break opposite at one of the most delightful eateries in this area, Kechmara (▷ 92), a great place any time of the day.

⑤ Cross over Avenue Mohamed V, where Place Vendome is on the corner and continue down Rue de la Liberté—with its boutiques and restaurants–to shop for gifts at Côté Sud (▷ 90).

Shopping

BAZAAR ATLAS

Pieces of art and jewellery created by the Berbers of the nearby Atlas Mountains are on sale here. There's a great selection and most of the assistants speak good English.

✚ C3 ✉ 129 imm. Gidel, Avenue Mohamed V, Guéliz ☎ No phone

CÔTÉ SUD

The three levels of this small shop are full of contemporary Moroccan delights for the home, such as orange sorbet candles, pretty silk cushion covers and funky coloured tin chandeliers. This tiny emporium is a real gem: If you only make it to one shop in Guéliz, make it this one.

✚ C3 ✉ 4 Rue de la Liberté, Guéliz ☎ 024 438 448

JEFF DE BRUGES

Exquisite, Belgian-style chocolates are sold by the weight and they don't come cheap—about 55 dirhams (€5) for a 100g bag. Speciality chocolates in the shape of rabbits and ducklings particularly appeal to little ones.

✚ C3 ✉ 17 Rue de la Liberté, Guéliz ☎ 024 430 249

INTENSITÉ NOMADE

If you are after couture kaftans with upbeat designs, or even one in camouflage print, this is the place to come.

Designer Frédérique Birkemeyer is something of a legend in the city and this is a fun spot to stop purely to window shop.

✚ C3 ✉ 70 Rue de la Liberté, Guéliz ☎ 024 431 333

MAISON ROUGE

Fine interior furnishings on several floors, including embroidered curtains, highly decorative candle holders and colourful textiles for both bedroom and lounge.

✚ C3 ✉ 6 Rue de la Liberté, Guéliz ☎ 024 448 130

MICHELE BACONNIER

Original designs and modern takes on Moroccan favourites, including jewellery, lanterns and bags.

✚ C3 ✉ 6 Rue du Vieux, Guéliz ☎ 024 449 178

THE BEST OF BOTH WORLDS

Fixed prices, air-conditioned shops and smiling, efficient and knowledgeable shop assistants are some of the appeals of shopping in the New City. It is a world away from the dusty crowded souks, where the need to bargain stretches out the simple purchase and often leaves you feeling ripped off. That said, don't be afraid to try a bit of haggling in the boutiques of Guéliz—old habits die hard.

MYSHA AND NITO

High fashion, expensive costume jewellery and valuable art objects are the offerings here, appealing to local ladies who lunch, as well as a fair share of well-heeled international tourists.

✚ C3 ✉ Rue Sourya with corner of Tarrik Ibn Ziyad, Guéliz ☎ 824 42 16 38

L'ORIENTALISTE

Beautifully decorated bottles, artisan pieces of pottery, tea glasses and bowls. Reasonable prices; great for gifts.

✚ C3 ✉ 15 Rue de la Liberté, Guéliz ☎ 024 437 074

PLACE VENDOME

Desirable soft leather bags, wallets and jackets, all stylishly designed. Prices, however, would not be out of place in Paris.

✚ C3 ✉ 141 Avenue Mohamed V, Guéliz ☎ 024 435 263

SCENES DE LIN

Textiles and linens in lovely colours and embroidered cushions are some of the pretty and practical items on sale here.

✚ C3 ✉ 70 Rue de la Liberté, Guéliz ☎ 024 436 108

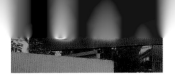

Entertainment and Activities

Nightlife

COLEUR POURPRE
One of the newest clubs in the city, but looks set to become a long-standing favourite. Cocktail lounge, tapas, live music and shows, DJ, karaoke—take your pick.
➕ B2 ✉ 7 Rue Ibn Zaydoun, Guéliz
☎ 024 437 302

NIKKI BEACH
www.nikkibeach.com
This club/bar/restaurant complex is already successful in Miami and St. Tropez. Day visitors pose on Balinese beds at the swim-up cocktail bar and in the lagoon-shaped pool. Young, fashion-conscious Moroccans wearing skimpy bikinis knock back European-priced champagne, hidden from the rest of Muslim Marrakech and its traditional values.
➕ Off map ✉ Nikki Beach, Circuit de la Palmeraie
☎ 024 368 727

PACHA
www.pachamarrakech.com
Well-known Ibiza nightclub, Pacha, has been brought to Morocco, and its creators boast it is the biggest club in Africa. Revellers come dressed to impress, chilling out in the lounge and by the pool (open only in fine weather), or to eat in one of the restaurants. Mostly though, as with all the Pacha clubs, they come to dance to the sounds of internationally famed DJs.
➕ Off map ✉ Avenue Mohamed VI ☎ 024 388 400

THEATRO
www.theatromarrakech.com
The opulent interior of this former theatre is now a nightclub. Ladies', Ministry of Sound and theme nights. Performers fill the large, galleried space and their attempts to make this an experience do work; one of the most enjoyable clubs in Marrakech.
➕ D7 ✉ Hotel Es Saadi, Avenue El Qadissia ☎ 024 448 811

Sports and Activities

DUNES & DESERT EXPLORATION
www.dunesdesert.com
Thrilling half-day go-karting and quad biking trips and camel rides through a landscape of dried out rivers, palm trees and Berber villages—though not strictly desert.
➕ Off map ✉ Hôtel Club Palmariva, Km 6, Route de Fès
☎ 061 246 948

OASIRIA WATER PARK
Slide down the giant toboggans, float down the river, splash about in the enormous wave pool and surrender to the thrilling Somersault. The swimming pool and one of two children's lagoons offer calmer entertainment. There is also a volley ball court, pirate ship and restaurant.
➕ Off map ✉ Oasiria, Km 4, Route de Barrage ☎ 024 380 438 🚌 Free Shuttle service

ROYAL GOLF COURSE
Built in 1923, the oldest course in Morocco and superior to the other two 18-hole courses (at the time of writing, several more championship courses were being built). Well maintained, if rather uniform, course where royalty and Churchill have putted.
➕ Off map ✉ BP 634 Ancienne Route de Ouarzazate ☎ 024 404 705

UP TO THE MINUTE
The New City becomes ever newer by the minute. This is the place to come for 21st-century cosmopolitan entertainment. It can be a struggle to get even a beer in the medina, but in Guéliz and surrounds it's a different matter. Think of Las Vegas with an eastern twist: Casinos, bars, belly dancing and nightclubs that don't close until dawn, are all here.

THE NEW CITY

ENTERTAINMENT AND ACTIVITIES

Restautants

PRICES

Prices are approximate, based on a 3-course meal for one person.

€€€	over €40
€€	€20–€40
€	under €20

L'ABYSSIN (€€€)

www.restaurant-labyssin.com
Where celebs such as the Beckhams might eat if they were in town. Unashamedly over-the-top restaurant and open air cocktail bar with beds by the pool. French nouvelle cuisine, but the experience is more memorable than the food. Groups of diners are hosted in white tents, while couples are given romantic, candle-lit poolside tables. Plan on spending the whole evening here, drinking and lounging as well as dining.
➕ Off map ✉ Km 6, Palais Rhoul Route de Fes, La Palmeraie ☎ 024 328 584
🕐 Daily 7pm–late

LE BAGATELLE (€€)

Good, traditional French bistro fare has been served at this restaurant since 1949. Feast on duck or steak on the delightful terrace.
➕ B4 ✉ 101 Rue de Yougoslavie, Guéliz
☎ 024 430 274
🕐 Thu–Tue 12–2.30, 7–12

BÔ-ZIN (€€–€€€)

www.bo-zin.com
There's a noticeably Thai accent on the food here, with Italian and French food, too. The reason to come, though, is to dine and dance in a beautiful garden setting. One of the best night's out in the city. Dress to impress and plan on staying until dawn. Reservations are essential. Also plan on taking a taxi there and back as it's quite a way out of the city centre.
➕ Off map ✉ Douar Lahna, Km 3.5 Route de l'Ourika ☎ 024 388 012
🕐 Daily 7pm–late

LE COMPTOIR DARNA (€€€)

www.comptoirdarna.com
Another restaurant where the main draw is the experience rather than the nouvelle cuisine food. Probably the most recommended restaurant in the city, mostly because of its good performances

THE FRENCH FACTOR

Although the influence of the French colonialists can be felt all over town, it is in the new city's slick continental-style brasseries and European coffee shops that it is most keenly felt. One of the pleasures of this part of Marrakech is chowing down on succulent steaks, quaffing fine wines and spending the day doing nothing more than sipping on strong, dark coffee, perhaps soaking it up with a buttery croissant.

by belly dancers (at 10.30pm). Insist on a table in the main room. Reservations essential.
➕ E6 ✉ Avenue Echouhada, Hivernage
☎ 024 437 702
🕐 Daily 7pm–late

KECHMARA (€–€€)

www.kechmara.com
There isn't a bad time to come here; breakfast (orchid oolong tea, delicious crêpes), lunch of a roast beef sandwich or warm goats cheese salad and dinner (international, daily changing menu) are all enjoyable. The minimalist interior, smooth music and excellent food always draw the crowds.
➕ C3 ✉ 3 Rue de la Liberté, Guéliz ☎ 024 422 532 🕐 Mon–Sat 7pm–midnight

LOLO QUOI (€€)

A stylish, seductive bar and restaurant, where the lighting is low and the food rich (mostly meat and pasta) but consistently good. Try a succulent fillet steak the size of your fist with pasta gratin.
➕ C4 ✉ 82 Avenue Hassan II ☎ 072 569 864
🕐 Mon–Sat 12–3, 7–midnight

LE PALAIS JAD MAHAL (€€€)

Dining here is like eating in a Parisian palace with Indian-inspired decor. High quality French-Moroccan food, accompanied by belly dancers. There's a bar at the back and a DJ

starts up around midnight. Reservations essential.

🚇 E7 ✉ 10 Rue Haroun Errachid, Hivernage ☎ 024 436 984 🕐 Daily 8pm–2am

RESTAURANT AL FASSIA (€€€)

www.alfassia.com
A favourite with locals and visitors alike. Superb, home-cooked food (à la carte Moroccan) served in formal surroundings. A women's cooperative, where the chefs, waiting staff and even the management are all female. Reservations essential.

🚇 B3 ✉ 55 Boulevard Mohamed Zerktouni, Guéliz ☎ 024 434 060 🕐 Tue–Sun 12–2.30, 7.30–11

ROTISSERIE DE LA PAIX (€€)

The garden of the 'Rotisserie of Peace' is particularly lovely at night when it is candle-lit. Juicy charcoaled meats and winning *plats du jours* have been satisfying visitors since 1949.

🚇 C4 ✉ 68 Rue Yougoslavie, Guéliz ☎ 024 433 118 🕐 Daily 12–3, 6–11

Cafés

CAFÉ DU LIVRE

www.cafedulivre.com
Expats and jaded tourists come here for Wi-Fi, English books and magazines as well as the light, international menu created by two Michelin star chef, Richard Neat.

🚇 C3 ✉ 44 rue Tarrik Ibn

Ziyad, Guéliz (entrance via Hotel Toulousain) ☎ 024 432 149 🕐 Mon–Sat 9.30am–9pm

CAFÉ EXTRABLATT

A successful German franchise has brought café, bar, restaurant and disco under one roof. Take tea on the terrace of Café Extrablatt; drink cocktails in the Artemis lounge before dinner in the Italian restaurant and move onto the disco at Be One (from 11pm).

🚇 E6 ✉ Corner of Avenue Echouhada with Rue Alkadissia, next to Darna Comptoir, Hivernage ☎ 024 434 843 🕐 Terrace café 7am–midnight; restaurant daily 6pm–1am

GRAND CAFÉ DE LA POSTE

www.grandcafedelaposte.com
Built in 1925, and beautifully renovated in

CAFÉ SOCIETY

The cafés in the New City are much, much more than a place to have a cappuccino. As in Paris, they are at the literary and cultural heart of this part of the town; places to see and be seen in, venues for business meetings, and locations of romantic liaisons. Opening first thing in the morning and often not closing until the early hours of the next, the New City's cafés offer all-hours respite from the rest of the city.

the style of a Parisian brasserie, this café oozes old world glamour. By day, coffees and salads are served under white parasols on the breezy terrace. At night, sink into a red velvet sofa with a cocktail, soothed by live jazz and tuck into golden chicken with thyme or tender pink duck breast. This café really is grand, as well as being a delightful spot to spend an hour to two, it perfectly epitomizes the successful fusion of history and modernity in the New City.

🚇 C4 ✉ Corner of Boulevard El Mansour Eddahbi and Avenue Imam Malik, Guéliz ☎ 024 433 038 🕐 🕐 Daily 8am–1pm

JARDIN MAJORELLE CAFÉ

www.jardinmajorelle.com
Deep in the Majorelle Gardens (▷ 82–83) is this pretty patio café dripping with bougainvillea. Iced milk with orange blossom, old-fashioned lemonade and chilled tomato gazpacho are cooling delights, with chocolate pancakes and banana splits sweet enticements. These treats make it a good place to bring children, and if it rains there is comfortable seating inside. This is one of the highlights of the gardens; so try and fit in a visit.

🚇 E2 ✉ Avenue Yacoub el Mansour, Guéliz ☎ 024 301 852 🕐 Jun–end Sep daily 8–6; Oct–end May daily 8–5

Less than an hour's drive south or east of the city, the ascent begins into the Atlas Mountains, a region of soaring peaks and fertile valleys dotted with Berber villages. A three-hour drive west of Marrakech is the coastal resort of Essaouira—a lovely, laid-back beach destination.

Essaouira

HIGHLIGHTS

● Craft shops and art galleries
● Sandy beaches
● Relaxed nightlife
● *Gnawa* music festival in June

TIPS

● Take an evening stroll to Borj El Berod, an evocative, crumbling old fort at the far end of the main beach.
● Head to the old fashioned port around 3pm for an open air, grilled fish lunch.

This pretty port town is just a three-hour drive from Marrakech. Its beaches attract a mixture of wind surfers, artists, hippies and chilled-out young holidaymakers escaping the dust of the desert city.

A breath of fresh air Two or three days here adds an extra dimension to any Marrakech break. Expect freshly caught fish, a rich musical heritage and a relaxed take on the Islamic way of life. The traditional medina and rampart walls are here, but within are streets laid out on a European grid with whitewashed buildings and azure blue shutters. Stroll the cobbled streets and you will find hidden cafés, restaurants, galleries and craft shops. Head to the workshops built into the town's western sea wall, known as Skala de la Ville. Here you will

Clockwise from far left: sandy beach and view toward Essaouira; clocktower and gate, Avenue Okba Nafia; away from the crowds at the beach; highly decorative doorways in the north of Essaouria town; view over the waves from Skala de la Ville ramparts at sunset

find the finest craftsmen in the country producing ornate wooden gifts and furniture.

Beachside On the south edge of the town is a wide and sandy playground for locals and tourists alike. Join in a game of football, laze around, or try your hand at windsurfing. For swimming, the northern beach, Plage de Safi, is quieter and calm if the winds are down (try to swim where and when the locals do).

Feast for the senses The main square, Moulay Hassan, is lined with pavement cafés, and it's tempting to spend the whole day here chatting, relaxing and people-watching. In June, the square is a key venue for the huge, fun *Gnawa* music festival (▷ 114).

THE BASICS

🞢 Off map to west
✉ Km 100 Route 207, leaving the N8 from Marrakech after 80km (50 miles)

Ourika Valley

HIGHLIGHTS

● Hiking up to a series of cascading waterfalls
● Paddling in the crystal clear pools formed by the mountain rivers

TIPS

● Bring supplies of water and sunblock, and wear a hat to protect yourself from the sun.
● Occasionally, locals construct a ramshackle open-air café at one of the pools, but bring your own snacks, too.

The Ourika River flows down through the foothills of the Atlas Mountains, giving life to this fertile valley. It's a wonderful daytrip from Marrakech, with the opportunity to relax in mountain pools and hike to pristine waterfalls.

On the road A grand taxi to the heart of the valley takes around an hour. Heading south from Marrakech the road rises into the hills from about the 30km (19 miles) mark. Berber families, clustered together in simple clay homes, have worked the land around here for centuries. Stop at the village of Aghbalou to see the unusual mosque built from mortared stone, like an English church.

Setti Fatma At the end of the paved road from Marrakech is this growing village where many

Clockwise from far top left: a view of the Ourika Valley near Tnine; mountain view near Setti Fatma; house in Setti Fatma; the Setti Fatma waterfalls; more colourful houses; crossing the Ourika river

locals have taken to the guide business. You'll meet plenty of them, offering to take you up to the waterfalls, but you can follow the rough tracks yourself—just make sure you wear stout shoes or hiking boots. The village itself is not particularly attractive, but if you're here in late August try and catch the *mousse*—a lively festival of music, dance and culture that lasts for three days.

Pools and falls In the hills above Setti Fatma, there are a total of seven waterfalls and pools where you can stop for a swim and a picnic. The path up is fairly narrow and the drops are steep, particularly beyond the second waterfall—those afraid of heights may wish to stop there. The adventurous may want to make a side trip to the ski-resort of Oukaïmedene. Take a left turn just after Aghbalou on the road back from Setti Fetma.

THE BASICS

➕ Off map to south
✉ Km 60, Route S513, Ourika Valley
🚌 Grand taxis (▷ 118) leave from Marrakech all morning, and return from Setti Fatma late in the evening.
🍴 Good food in Café Asgaour overlooking the river in Setti Fatma
❓ Guides will look to charge between 170 dirhams (€15) and 225 dirhams (€20) to take you up to the waterfalls

Tizi-n-Test

HIGHLIGHTS

● The exciting drive through the mountains, with views to die for
● Mule treks in the woods around Ourigane

TIPS

● Driving in the mountains is not for the faint-hearted, so join an organized tour, or simply hire a grand taxi (▷ 118).
● Plan on spending at least one night in the mountains, to avoid feeling rushed.

The Atlas Mountains offer much more than a pretty backdrop to Marrakech. Hit the road south from the city to experience the drama of high mountain passes, memorable views, country pursuits and out-of-town hospitality.

Tizi heights Historically, control of the Atlas hinged on a few key *tizis* (mountain passes). In the 1920s, the French cut a new road through this pass, effectively stripping the Berber tribes of their access to the south and control of this mountainous region. The Tizi-n-Test road, 50km (31 miles) south of Marrakech, begins its rise into the mountains. It is twisting and narrow, with fantastic, dizzying views across the Atlas Mountains. The small village of Ourigane is a good place for an overnight stay. Although not much in itself,

View of the Tizi-n-Test pass (far left); 4x4 cars taking the high road under the cliff overhang (left); Goundafi Kasbah on the Tizi-n-Test road (top right); spectacular views along the road (bottom left and right)

it is surrounded by pleasant orchards that invite evening strolls and daytime mule treks. Choose from Domaine Le Rosarie (▷ 110), a spa hotel on the edge of the town, or the more basic Dar Tassa (▷ 109) in the nearby hills. Both hotels will organize excursions to Tin Mal and other activities.

Mountain mosque In the 12th century, Tin Mal was a staging post in the Almohads' siege of Marrakech. The mosque here was built in 1153 and shortly afterwards defensive features were added to make the imposing fortress that still overlooks the pass. For non-Muslims, Tin Mal offers a rare chance to step inside a Moroccan mosque—the roof is gone, but much of the structure is remarkably well preserved. Today, there are a few houses and an olive press below the mosque by the riverside—nice for a picnic.

THE BASICS

Ourigane
🔛 Off map to south
✉ Km 60, R203 Route de Taroudant

Tin Mal
🔛 Off map to south
✉ Km 95, R203 Route de Taroudant

Tiz-n-Tichka

TOP 25

The fortified Aït Benhaddou (right) is fronted by the River Asif Mellah (left)

THE BASICS

🔲 Off map to south and southeast

Distance: 400km (248 miles) round trip from Marrakech, with overnight stay in Ouarzazate's Berber Palace (☎ 024 883 105; www.ouarzazate.com/leberberpalace)

🕐 Fortresses are open daily, during daylight hours

❓ Berber Tours (☎ 061 439 690; www.berbertours.net) offer 4x4 excursions to sights around Ouarzazate, as well as camel expeditions into the Sahara from 2 to 15 days

HIGHLIGHTS

● Berber market at Aït Ourir
● Mountain stronghold at Kasbah Telouet
● Famous film locations at Benhaddou and Ouarzazate

The Tiz-n-Tichka pass may be less a dramatic mountain drive than the Tizi-n-Test (▷ 102–103), but the sights are just as thrilling, including mountain fortresses and a desert outpost where you can spend the night.

Mountain stronghold Hire a grand taxi (▷ 118) for this trip, best begun on a Tuesday or Saturday when the Berber market at Aït Ourir (40km/25 miles from Marrakech) is in full swing. On from Aït Ourir (70km/43 miles) is the turn off for Kasbah Telouet. This was the mountain stronghold of the Glaoui brothers, fierce Berber leaders who ran large parts of the country up until 1956. Despite the medieval feel there was nothing here before the Glaoui brothers came in the late 19th century.

In the desert The evocative fortified desert town of Aït Benhaddou was famously used as a location in the film *Lawrence of Arabia* (1962). If you're in a grand taxi you'll need to hike the last 10km (6 miles) to the site, or you can join a 4x4 tour with Berber Tours in Ouarzazate, which is 30km (19 miles) farther along the main road.

Cinematic Ouarzazate was created by the French as a desert guard post but is now mainly known as the home of the Atlas Film Studios (☎ 022 541 556; www.atlasstudios.com), where you can see sets from epic movies such as *Gladiator* (2000) and *Star Wars* (1977). Today the city's 80,000 residents eke out a simple life when there are no filmmakers in residence.

More to See

JEBEL TOUBKAL

The ascent to the summit of North Africa's highest peak (4,147m/13,602 ft) is a once-in-a-lifetime opportunity for many people, and from June to September, after the snow has melted, you don't need to be an experienced climber—just reasonably fit. Plan on spending the night in the refuge at the 3,200m (10,496ft) snow line, before conquering the summit the next day, make sure someone knows where you are and be aware that you may have to wait for just the right weather.

🚩 Off map to south ✉ Access to the hiking paths from Imlil, 65km (40 miles) south of Marrakech 🍴 Dinner and a bed for the night in the CAF snow-line refuge will cost around 90 dirhams (€8) ❓ Good guides for the ascent can be found at the CAF (Club Alpin Français) refuge in Imlil (☎ 024 31 9036; www.caf-maroc.com), or you can ask for advice in Kasbah du Toubkal (▷ 109) 🖼 Plan on paying your guide 225–340 dirhams (€20–€30) per day.

LAKE TAKERKOUST

If you don't have time for an extended excursion, but would like a break from the dust and heat of Marrakech, try a daytrip to Lake Takerkoust, 30km (19 miles) from Marrakech. Dotted around the edge of this man-made lake are numerous restaurants and hotels, such as Relais du Lac, that double as activity centres for kayaking, jet-skis, or even horse riding or just for relaxing by the pool.

🚩 Off map to south ✉ Km30, Route S507 (from Marrakech turn off R203 to Taroudant after 8km/5 miles) 🍴 Relais du Lac (▷ 109)

A stream cutting through the mountains of Toubkal National Park

Snow-covered peak of Jebel Toubkal

Shopping

ARGAN OIL COOPERATIVES
The wonder beauty product that is argan oil is on sale from shops and market stalls in Essaouira, but stories abound that some of the bottles are little more than vegetable oil. To be sure that you are not only getting the real thing but that some of the profits are going to the women workers, buy argan oil that has been produced at a women's cooperative, either from shops in town or direct from coops on the Essaouira-Marrakech road.
➕ Off map ✉ Essaouira

GALERIE DAMGAARD
www.galeriedamgaard.com
There are countless small art galleries in Essaouira, which has drawn an artistic crowd since the 1950s. In Damgaard, works across the full spectrum are displayed and for sale, almost all by local artists.
➕ Off map ✉ Ave Oqba Nafiaa, Essaouira ☎ 024 784 446

Entertainment and Activities

BAR TAROS
The trendy rooftop café is a good place to hang out in the evenings for cocktails and tapas. It's on the main square and has live music some evenings.
➕ Off map ✉ 2 Rue du Skala, Essaouira ☎ 024 476 407

OCEAN VAGABOND
www.oceanvagabond.com
Windsurfing, surfing and kite surfing with or without instruction, as well as less serene and environmentally friendly quad biking from this nautical centre on the beach.
➕ Off map ✉ Boulevard Mohamed V, Essaouira ☎ 024 479 222

Restaurants

PRICES
Prices are approximate, based on a 3-course meal for one person.
€€€   over €40
€€   €20–€40
€   under €20

LES ALIZÉS (€)
Perhaps the most popular place in town. This is a simple, intimate restaurant with a relaxed atmosphere, serving excellent tasty traditional Moroccan cuisine.
➕ Off map ✉ 26 Rue de la Skala, Essaouira ☎ 024 476 819 🕒 Daily

LE CHALET DE LA PLAGE (€€)
The beachfront location is the main attraction of this long-standing restaurant; visit for a snack, seafood or pasta and admire the view. Reservations advised.
➕ Off map ✉ 1 Boulevard Mohamed V, Essaouira ☎ 024 475 972 🕒 Closed Sun and Mon lunch

LE CINQ (€€–€€€)
Part of the Madada Mogador (▷ 109) hotel, a contemporary offering with bright decor and modern Italian and French cuisine. Added bonuses are Wi-fi and occasional live music.
➕ Off map ✉ 7 Rue Youssef El Fassi, Essaouira ☎ 024 784 726 🕒 Closed Tue

FRESH FISH STALLS (€–€€)
At lunchtime get the daily catch—from sardines to lobster—of your choice cooked in front of you. Prices are given per kilo, so be on your guard and watch out for overcharging.
➕ Off map ✉ Entrance to the harbour, Essaouira ☎ No phone 🕒 Daily lunchtime

Whether you want a historic riad bursting with charm or a slick, state of the art international hotel with a swimming pool as large as a lake, Marrakech has it all. The city and its people are big on charm and your accommodation is one of the best places to enjoy it.

Introduction

There aren't many major sights in Marrakech. You will probably split your time between energetic morning bouts of souk-haggling and decadent evenings of fine cuisine, interspersed with hot, lazy afternoons enjoying a well-earned rest at your hotel. Accommodation in Marrakech is a little on the expensive side but bear in mind that each wonderfully unique riad hotel is a destination in itself.

Riad Regeneration

These Moroccan style boutique hotels often have just five or six rooms on two storeys around a central courtyard, but some are two or more houses knocked into one. Typically, they are restored historic buildings. Just 10 years ago, there were only a few hundred riads in Marrakech; today there are several thousand, which can make choosing one a bewildering experience. Most riads have rooftops terraces, few have vehicle access or pools big enough to swim in and the best offer an atmospheric oasis in the mayhem of the medina.

Modern Marrakech

Until now most of the international chain hotels were found in the New City district of Hivernage, but literally hundreds of 21st-century establishments are under construction in the outlying district of La Palmeraie. While many of them make a nod to Moorish design, and may even imitate the winning riad formula, few provide much real local flavour. There are mini-bars, room service, swimming pools and air-conditioning, but the experience can often feel impersonal and even bland.

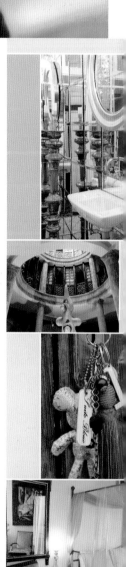

From the top: ornate bathroom; typical Marrakech hotel courtyard; room key detail, Marrakech-style; pleasant bedroom interior

PRICE HIKES

New City hotels and the medina's riads as much as double their prices at Christmas and Easter, with three or five night bookings often obligatory. Bear this in mind if you are enticed by cheap flights—at these times of year what starts off as a budget mini-break can easily end up breaking the bank.

Budget Hotels

PRICES

Expect to pay under €100 for a double room per night in a budget hotel.

DAR TASSA
www.dartassa.com
The two major draws of this place are the welcoming atmosphere and the panoramic views of the Toubkal National Park. Translating as 'mother love', this excellent value Berber guesthouse has friendly mountain guides and attentive service. Consider an overnight stay and a day trek with transport provided from Marrakech.
➕ Off map ✉ Douar Tassa, BP176, Ouirgane ☎ 079 886 081

JNANE MOGADOR
www.jnanemogador.com
A no-nonsense hotel and one of the best budget options, with consistently good feedback. Making a reservation is a bit of a trial though—push them for confirmation. Breakfast and dinner are extra. Hammam, rooftop with great views, and a great location minutes from Jemaa El Fna.
➕ J6 ✉ 116 Rue Riad Zitoun El Kédim, Derb Sidi Bouloukat ☎ 024 426 323

KASBAH DU TOUBKAL
www.kasbahdutoubkal.com
Accommodation in a dorm (suites are overpriced) in a restored mountain fortress. Only 40km (25 miles) from Marrakech, it's popular for day trips that include a visit to Imlil, the Kasbah for lunch and then a small Berber village. Longer packages available too. Works closely with the local community.
➕ Off map ✉ BP 31, Imlil ☎ (+44) 1883 744392 (from the UK)

MADADA MOGADOR
www.madada.com
One of Essouira's gems, stylish and with just seven spacious ensuite rooms, some with large baths. Panoramic views from the terrace looking out to sea. Friendly and efficient staff, delicious breakfasts and Wi-Fi.
➕ Off map ✉ 5 Rue Youssef el Fassi, Essaouira ☎ 024 475 512

HAVING IT ALL

Most of the smaller riads (with less than 8 rooms) will give you a special rate if you hire the whole building. This means you can have your own private residence for your family and friends at a discounted rate. This option has become increasingly popular for both extended family groups and friends who have clubbed together for special occasions; the experience is unforgettable.

RELAIS DU LAC
www.aubergedulac-marrakech.com
Basic but pleasant lakeside villa, where you can stop for lunch or dinner, or spend a night or two and include canoe trips on the lake and hikes around the shore. The rooms are functional, but the food is tasty and good value. For a fun evening, you can spend the night in a Bedouin tent by the lake.
➕ Off map ✉ Relais du Lac, BP 44 Route d'Azizmizmiz, C/R Lalla takerkoust ☎ 024 484 924 /061 187 472

RIAD ARIHA
www.riadariha.com
Reliable and excellent value for this price bracket. Minimalist Moroccan where all the rooms are named after plants. Plunge pools, hammam and massage, but most of all incredibly friendly staff.
➕ H2 ✉ Sidi bin Slimane, Kaa Sour, 90 Derb Ahmed el Borj ☎ 024 375 850

RIAD HIDA
www.riadhida.com
Highly recommended and excellent value. Lovely peacock-filled gardens, pool, spectacular interior and really good food. So welcoming and relaxing, most people don't want to leave.
➕ Off map ✉ Ouled Berhil, Route de Taroudant ☎ 048 531 044

Mid-Range Hotels

PRICES

Expect to pay between €100 and €200 per night for a double room in a mid-range hotel.

BELDI COUNTRY CLUB

www.beldicountryclub.com
Just outside of Marrakech, it mimics the ancient *douar* (Moroccan hamlet) style, with gardens, terraces and a lake-like pool surrounded by olive and palm trees. Excellent cuisine.

➕ Off map ✉ Km 6, Route du Barrage, Cherifia ☎ 024 383 950

CARAVANSERAI

www.caravanserai.com
On the fringes of La Palmeraie, an effortlessly stylish, rustic resort with rooms around a patio garden. Relax in the heated pool (open to day guests), or go camel trekking or quad biking in the surrounding countryside.

➕ Off map ✉ 24 Ouled Ben Rahmoune, La Palmeraie ☎ 024 300 302

CASA LALLA

www.casalalla.com
This minimalist riad is very reasonably priced. French owned, although the Michelin chef is long gone and the breakfasts tend to be rather basic. Avoid the rooms on the ground floor that get the noise of breakfast and dinner guests.

➕ J6 ✉ 16 Derb Jamaa, Rue Riad Zitoun El Kédim ☎ 024 429 757

CASA TAOS

www.casataos.net
Grand house with gardens and large swimming pool. Rooms inspired by famous artists. The prettiest suite, with pink and blue decor, is named after Mexican artist Frida Kahlo. Like most hotels out of the medina, a place to relax, perhaps combined with a few days in the city itself.

➕ Off map ✉ Km 8, Route de Souilha ☎ 061 200 414

DAR CHARKIA

www.darcharkia.com
Nothing is too much trouble for the owners and staff of this riad, which offers a real home from home and a very comfortable stay. Heated swimming pool, pretty roof terrace and very good food.

➕ G4 ✉ 49–50 Derb Halfaoui, Bab Doukkala ☎ 024 376 477

A TIP OR TWO

Don't forget to leave a gratuity for your hotel chambermaid, and other staff who go the extra mile. The average annual wage in Morocco is little over 9,130 dirhams (around €800). In Morocco, it's standard practice to pay a little extra to get things done, so spread a little goodwill by giving tokens of your appreciation wherever you can.

DOMAINE LA ROSERAIE

www.laroseraiehotel.com
A lovely spot near the Tizi-n-Test pass. Visit for spectacular gardens surrounded by the High Atlas Mountains, relaxing by the pool and horse riding, rather than the rather bland rooms and down-at-heel spa services.

➕ Off map ✉ Km 60, Route de Taroudant, Ouirgane ☎ 024 485 693

L'HEURE D'ETÉ

www.lheure-dete.com
This is a no-frills, reasonably priced town house, but with too many rules and regulations. It is clean, and close to Jemaa El Fna, with breakfast served on the rooftop terrace.

➕ Off map ✉ 96 Sidi Bouloukat ☎ 024 391 727

RIAD HYATI

www.riadhayati.com
Partly because it only has three rooms, but also because it is a really beautiful riad with caring staff, Hyati is often fully booked. The 18th-century riad offers massages, guides and very good food.

➕ K7 ✉ 27 Derb Bouderba, Rue Riad Zitoun El Jedid, Marrakech Médina ☎ (+44) 7770 431 194 (from the UK)

RIAD KNIZA

www.riadkniza.com
The owners and staff of this gorgeous riad seem to genuinely care for their guests' welfare. One of

the few Moroccan-owned riads in Marrakech. Rate includes a half-day medina tour, and the optional mountain trips are recommended.

🔲 F4 ✉ 34 Derb L'Hotel, Bab Doukkala ☎ 024 376 942

RIAD LOTUS AMBRE

www.riadlotus.com
This is a slick, stylish operation with Indian-Syrian decor. A boutique hotel, even though there are several Riad Lotuses in the city. Attention to detail sometimes slips but generally good personal service.

🔲 H6 ✉ 22 Fbal Zafriti ☎ 024 431 537

RIAD MEHDI

www.riadmehdi.net
Great value and extremely comfortable, but book well in advance. All suite accommodation, the lounges are air-conditioned, and there's a spa, garden and pool. With such attention to architectural detail, it's really hard to tell it's a new build.

🔲 H8 ✉ 2 Derb Sedra, Bab Agnaou ☎ 024 384 713/717

RIAD NOGA

www.riadnoga.com
As homely as an English bed-and-breakfast, complete with cascading bougainvillea and tea, coffee and slippers in the rooms. The pool (large for a riad), roof terrace and deep, mosaic baths

are a real draw. Appeals to older visitors and those with older children. Closed August.

🔲 K6 ✉ 78 Rue Douar Graoua ☎ 024 377 670

RIAD SLITINE

www.riad-slitine.com
Just two minutes from the main square is this spacious, 17th-century riad and gardens. Although there is heating, it can get cold at night. The larger pool can actually be used for swimming—almost unique in the medina.

🔲 J6 ✉ Rue Riad Zitoun El Jedid, 42 Derb Zenka Deika ☎ 024 385 810

RIAD TIZWA

www.riadtizwa.com
A simply charming and relaxed, very reasonably

RIAD RESERVATIONS

Most people come home raving about their Marrakech riad—a haven in the sprawling bustle of the medina. However, they may not suit everyone. Rooms open directly onto shared courtyards, so don't expect total privacy. Service can sometime be lackadaisical, compared to the 5-star New City experience, and the pool is normally more of a plunge bath. If you have young children, then a riad, with its steep stairs, sharp corners and delicate objets d'art, probably isn't for you.

priced riad. Consider booking Room 2—on its own on the roof terrace, or Room 3 with its en-suite hammam. All rooms have iPod docking stations. Stay in bed all day if you like—the lovely breakfast is served any time up until supper.

🔲 G4 ✉ 26 Derb Gueraba, Dar el Bacha ☎ 068 190 872

RIAD 72

www.riad72.com
Delightful, Italian-run riad, with charming service. Just four rooms, including a bridal suite; the whole place can be rented for as little as 6,850 dirhams (around €600). Enjoy the wonderful food, and relax in the hammam or under the banana trees. Good deals for families.

🔲 G4 ✉ 72 Arset Awsel, Bab Doukkala ☎ 024 387 629

VILLA LOTUS EVA

www.riadslotus.com
With just five rooms, this place offers the romantic intimacy of a riad, but the quiet and comfort of a hotel outside the medina. All rooms have mini bars, hi-fis and microwaves. Price deals for families and cots are available.

🔲 D7 ✉ Fbal Zefriti, Hivernage ☎ 024 431 537

Luxury Hotels

PRICES

Expect to pay more than €200 per night for a double room in a luxury hotel.

BERBERE PALACE

www.ouarzazate.com/leberberepalace

On the expensive side, but then this is five-star luxury. The charming pool offers welcome relief from the heat, and there are a host of activities to chose from, including desert 4x4 trips.

➕ Off map ✉ Quartier Mansour Eddahbi, Ouarzazate ☎ 024 883 105

LES JARDINS DE LA KOUTOUBIA

www.lesjardinsdelakoutoubia.com

One of the few places to stay in the old town that offers luxurious, yet child friendly, accommodation. Charming staff, three swimming pools and three great restaurants. Spa open to non-guests.

➕ H6 ✉ 26 Rue El Koutoubia ☎ 024 388 800

MAISON MNABHA

www.maisonmnabha.com

There is nothing lacking in this 17th-century palace filled with antiques. It boasts satellite TV and five-star luxury. Real attention to detail, highly personal service and excellent meals.

➕ J9 ✉ 32-33 Derb Mnabha, Kasbah ☎ 024 381 325

RIAD AL MASSARAH

www.riadalmassarah.com

The pool and serene cream courtyard is breathtakingly beautiful. In some style-heavy riads comfort is sacrificed, but here there are real fires and warm duvets. Wi-Fi, hammam, massage and a superb chef. The owners invest in their staff—giving a good level of service.

➕ G4 ✉ 26 Derb Djedid, Bab Doukkala ☎ 024 383 206

RIAD ENIJA

www.riadenija.com

Wonderfully eclectic —many of the carved wooden doors and lamps are actually from India— and a magical place to stay. Dining in the garden is truly enchanting. The pool is rather tucked away and there's no hamman, but the massages are sublime. No credit cards.

➕ J5 ✉ 9 Derb Mesfioui, Place Rabba Kédim ☎ 024 440 926

NEWER THAN NEW

The New City gets newer every minute, with more than 100 large international resorts currently under construction. Worldwide chains don't offer much local flavour, but there is something alluring about air-conditioned pavilions, and private infinity pools. More and more visitors enjoy the best of both worlds, with a two-centre break that combines a few days in the old city with a few more in the new.

RIAD FARNATCHI

www.riadfarnatchi.com

Book suite 1 for your very own mini riad and be soothed by the sound of your private fountain. Enjoy a candle-lit supper or a barbecue for two on the roof, snuggle up in one of the *b'hous* (covered sitting areas), or get scrubbed down in the hammam. The service puts this riad in a league of its own.

➕ J4 ✉ Derb el Farnatchi, Rue Souk el Fassis, Qua'at Ben Ahid ☎ 024 384 910/912

LA SULTANA DE LA MEDINA

www.lasultanamarrakech.com

Live like royalty in the heart of the Kasbah. Aim for a luxury suite with fireplace and marble bathroom, and lounge in the heated pool, spa and Jacuzzi. This hotel is a deserved member of the Great Hotels of the World group. It also has taxi access.

➕ H8 ✉ 403 Rue de la Kasbah ☎ 024 388 008

VILLA DES ORANGERS

www.villadesorangers.com

This is an old Marrakech favourite. Just six rooms but, as in many riads, each varies hugely in size, decor and price. Excellent food in one of Morocco's few Relais and Châteaux restaurants, and it also has a pool.

➕ H7 ✉ 6 Rue Sidi Mimoun, Place Ben Tachfine ☎ 024 384 638

Marrakech can be a challenging city and most visitors only have a few days to enjoy it. Follow this guide to planning and travel that includes essential facts, some key words and phrases and a potted history.

Planning Ahead

When to Go

Marrakech really is a year-round destination, apart from the months of July and August, which are prohibitively hot. Most people will find winter warm enough, and even then there are hot afternoons that limit the amount of walking you can sensibly manage. Temperatures are usually at least several degrees cooler in the mountains and in breezy Essaouira.

TIME

L Marrakech is on GMT, but clocks don't go forward in summer. From March to October it is one hour behind London and four ahead of New York.

AVERAGE DAILY MAXIMUM TEMPERATURES

JAN	FEB	MAR	APR	MAY	JUN	JUL	AUG	SEP	OCT	NOV	DEC
64°F	68°F	73°F	79°F	84°F	91°F	100°F	100°F	91°F	82°F	73°F	66°F
18°C	20°C	23°C	26°C	29°C	33°C	38°C	38°C	33°C	28°C	23°C	19°C

Temperatures shown are the average daily maximum for each month.

Spring Early spring is a pleasant time to visit the city and not too hot.
Summer The summer months are unbearably hot, and therefore not a good time to visit the city.
Autumn Late autumn is a good time to visit.
Winter Rainfall is very low in Marrakech but when a winter downpour comes the streets get muddy. Hikers and visitors to the mountains should check snowfall, which regularly restricts access to certain routes.

WHAT'S ON

January *Marrakech International Marathon*: Worldwide athletes mix with local/charity runners (www.marathon-marrakech.com).
February *Dakka Marrakchia Festival*, Marrakech: A 5-day festival aimed at reviving a 1,000 year-old tradition, with musical performances.
May *Alizés Musical Spring Festival*, Essaouira: Four days of orchestral performances, chamber music and opera (www.alizesfestival.com).
June *Festival of Gnawa and World Music*, Essaouira: Five days of uplifting and interesting music (www.festival-gnaoua.co.ma).
July *Marrakech Popular Arts Festival*: Musicians, dancers, and acrobats from all over Morocco and beyond.
August *Imilchil Marriage Feast*, High Atlas: Berber tradition in which elaborate public courtships lead up a day of multiple weddings. Music, dance and a bustling market.
September/October *Ramadan*: Sacred month of Islam with daily fasting, and special attention to the Koran's teachings.

Non-Muslim visitors should make particular efforts not to cause offence. Don't smoke or eat in the street before sunset, don't use bad language, and dress modestly (men and women).
October *Festival of the Atlantic Andalusias*, Essaouira: A mainly musical affair celebrating the cultural contribution of Andalusia.
November/December *International Film Festival*, Jemaa El-Fna: Showcasing world cinema attracting visiting stars (www.festivalmarrakech.net).

Useful Websites

www.visitmorocco.org
The official site of the Moroccan Tourist Board has sketchy information about the mountain areas surrounding Marrakech, as well as the city itself. The directory of agents around the world providing travel to Morocco is perhaps the most useful segment.

www.ilove-marrakesh.com
'I Love Marrakesh' is a commercial site carrying advertising. Aimed at tourists, it concentrates on the most popular attractions, restaurants, shopping, arts and crafts etc. Its sister site, www.ilove-essaouira.com. covers the seaside resort in a similar fashion.

www.ilovemarrakech.com
A poor imitation of the above site, but may be worth a look if you are after self-catering accommodation or business news.

www.tourism-in-morocco.com
Laid out something like a blog, this guide to the whole of the country is well written but unfortunately badly organized, and several of the links don't function.

www.morocco.com
There is plenty of content on this site, which describes itself as a 'gathering place' but the quality of submissions (anyone can contribute) is inevitably variable. Listings of self-catering apartments in Marrakech, business news, and interesting blogs are some of the reasons to visit.

http://thehouseinmarrakesh.blogspot.com
Expat blog about daily life and decor in Marrakech, with great photographs. Intelligent and thoughtful, this is a step up from the shallow and self-congratulatory 'My Marrakesh' (http://moroccanmaryam.typepad.com) that seems to get much more publicity.

GETTING CONNECTED

Just about every riad, most hotels and even most hostels offer an internet service to their guests, and it is usually cheaper and more convenient than finding an internet café. Wi-Fi connections, for use with your own laptop, are increasingly common and there is often a computer reserved for guests to access the Internet. On some keyboards, tourists have problems obtaining the '@' symbol–you may have to hold down the 'Alt Gr' key to obtain it.

CYBER PARK

Wi-Fi zone with internet terminals in a royal park. ⊠ Moulay Abdeslam Cyber Park, Avenue Mohamed V, (entrance opposite Ensemble Artisanal) ⊠ No phone; www.arsatmoulayabdeslam.ma 🕐 Daily 9am–7pm 🎫 Free

A MOVABLE FEAST

Like other Islamic festivals, the holy month of Ramadan (▷ 114) is a movable feast, around 11 days earlier each successive year in the Western calendar. Visit during Ramadan and you will find some shops and attractions closing at irregular hours, as the Islamic people concentrate on prayer and contemplation.

Getting There

ENTRY REQUIREMENTS

All visitors, whatever their nationality, must have a passport that is valid for at least six months from the date of entry. Most nationalities, including British, German and American do not need a visa, but regulations can change so always check well before you travel. Onward or return tickets and inoculations are not required. These requirements apply to visits of three months or less. Ensure your passport is stamped upon arrival. If the stamp is missing, it can cause problems with Passport Control on your departure.

AIRPORT

Menara Airport (RAK) is just 6km (4 miles) from the city centre. There are two terminals (☎ 024 447 910, www.onda.org.ma). Car rental is available in the terminal. There are the usual services including shopping and restaurants.

90 miles (150km)

Casablanca Airport
(76 miles from Marrakech)

Marrakech
Marrakech Airport (Ménara)

FROM MENARA AIRPORT

To reach the city from the airport take a 15-minute taxi ride, or by number 11 and 19 buses, which take around 30 minutes. It is well worth having your riad or hotel pre-arrange a transfer from Marrakech's Menara airport. You probably won't pay any more than if you try to negotiate on arrival, as the taxi drivers operate something of a cartel. Best of all, your pre-arranged driver will know how to reach your riad or hotel—no mean feat in the medina.

ARRIVING BY AIR

For full-service flights from the UK and continental Europe, look at Iberia (www.iberia.com) and the national airline Royal Air Maroc (www.royalairmaroc.com). RAM also flies from New York stopping off in Casablanca, and their no-frills subsidiary Atlas Blue (www.atlas-blue.com) flies direct to Marrakech from many European hubs. Other European budget options include Easyjet (www.easyjet.com), Ryanair (www.ryanair.com), Thomsonfly (www.thomsonfly.com), Jet4You (www.jet4you.com) and TUI (www.tuifly.com).

ARRIVING BY BUS

Eurolines (www.eurolines.co.uk) operate services form mainland Europe and Britain to Marrakech and to Essaouira. You will be on the bus for upwards of a couple of days.

ARRIVING BY CAR

Few drivers will arrive by car, but if you do have a vehicle in Morocco drive on the right, and observe the following speed limits, as well as any signed restrictions:
Built-up areas: 50kph (30mph)
Highways: 100kph (60mph)

Watch out for vehicles with no lights, mopeds and bikes at night. You will need to bring you own child seats. Try to avoid car rental. Driving in the city of Marrakech is not for the faint-hearted, and driving into the mountains is positively frightening. You can hire a car with a driver for just a little more than a car alone. If you're determined, there are plenty of car hire companies at the airport and in Guéliz.

ARRIVING BY RAIL

A rail journey from Europe will take you south to the Spanish port of Algeciras and after the ferry crossing to Tangier (www.trasmediter-ranea.es), south again to Marrakech with ONCF railways (www.oncf.ma). To plan your route from a European capital, visit www.seat61.com. Inter-rail cards (for those under 26 years of age) are valid for use in Morocco.

Old Marrakech is not a great place to bring young children; there are few things to entertain them and it's difficult to get around with a buggy. Families are best off in one of the hotels with better facilities outside of the medina. The medina's riads really aren't suitable, because of their precious decor and intimate, echoing space. Try a New City hotel with short visits to the medina, followed by a trip to the mountains or sea (▷ 98–105).

Make sure your travel insurance package includes a minimum of 2.5 million euros towards medical treatment, including provision to fly you home in the case of an emergency. If you go abroad twice or more each year, an annual travel insurance policy might be the best value. Don't rely on the inclusive insurance provided with credit cards, as this very rarely provides sufficient cover. Travel insurance really is essential, and many agencies and airlines insist on it as a matter of course. Don't leave home without it.

Getting Around

HUSTLERS

Avoid those boys and young men who approach you in the street to assist with directions. Although almost certainly harmless, they will want to charge you for directions or guidance, and might waste your time with a painful detour to their 'uncle's shop'. If you do get lost, don't panic and don't wander around looking desperate. Ask a shopkeeper, or pick out a local who is not obviously vying for your attention, and ask them to help.

GUIDES

In the past a guide would most certainly have been a good idea, if simply to keep the hustlers off your back. However, police crackdowns have now made this largely unnecessary. If you do want a guide, get your hotel to recommend one, or get a licensed guide from the tourist office. Always agree a price beforehand, and be aware that they may get hefty commissions from certain shops.

BUSES

With taxis abundant and cheap, few travellers use public transport, but for those on a budget or eager to plunge into local life, there is a public bus system. Do watch out for pickpockets but don't become overly paranoid. The #1 bus will take you to Guéliz in the New City. The #8 runs to the train station and the #10 to the coach station, while the #11 heads southwest to the airport, stopping at the Menara Gardens.

TAXIS

Always agree a price first, as most drivers refuse to use their meters with tourists. Before you depart, ensure the driver clearly understands your destination, and don't be afraid to get out immediately if it looks like he has no idea where you want to go.

Grand taxis These are bigger cars, usually Mercedes, and serve as collective taxis for up to five people. They are not much use if you are going deep into the old town, as they are limited to the big streets at the edge of the medina. For a group of four people these are often better value than two petit taxis, and are a good alternative to rental cars for journeys out of the city.

Petit taxis These are small yellow hatch-backs with meters, though you will often have to agree a price due to a broken meter. It is cheaper to hail one in the street than from a hotel or restaurant, although the doorman will often communicate your destination better than you can. Even petit taxis will only

get you so far in the medina, so be prepared to do a bit of walking, and remember: no more than three passengers per car.

TOUR BUSES

A red double-decker bus is a strange sight in Marrakech and one you certainly can't fail to spot. Although more of a tour than public transport, the 24-hour hop-on hop-off ticket makes this a useful way for newcomers to get their bearings, particularly with the multi-lingual recorded information system.

The buses operate two different routes. 'Marrakech Monumental' visits the Theatre Royal, Palais des Congres, Place de la Liberté and Saâdien tombs, while the 'Romantique' route takes in Les Jardins Majorelle, Le Tikida Garden and Palmeraie Golf Palace. A recorded audio system provides tour highlights in any of eight languages, with the last bus running in the early evening most days.

WALKING IN THE MEDINA

Strolling around the ancient medina, you might feel almost perpetually lost, but this is all part of the fun. With twisting narrow alleyways and confusingly similar intersections, a compass might come in handy, but many prefer to wander aimlessly and be surprised by the city's delights. Those with young children should try to avoid the medina on foot, with its buzzing scooters and plodding donkeys, uneven walkways and often searing heat. Older children, around ten and up tend to appreciate the medieval feel, and strange sights, smells and sounds. The medina is encircled by the old city walls. Walking beyond the walls is like hiking along the side of a dusty motorway, and there are few concessions to pedestrians.

CALÈCHES

These open horse-drawn carriages are great if you want to soak up the sights and sounds of Marrakech on the move. Agree a price for your journey in advance, and don't expect to get anywhere in a hurry. They can also be rented by the hour (around 100 dirhams/€9 per hour) for sightseeing. The calèche stand is at Place Foucauld, just beyond the southwest corner of Jemaa El Fna.

VISITORS WITH DISABILITIES

Morocco lags behind many countries when it comes to providing disabled access and Marrakech can prove very challenging for anyone with mobility limitations— including those with a pushchair or pram. Even the large open main square of Jemma El Fna has uneven surfaces that can make travel with wheels a problem. That said, people are very willing to help and the newer hotels —of which there are many— are much better equipped. If you do have a disability, make full enquiries with your agent or hotel before you make any booking.

Essential Facts

EMERGENCY NUMBERS

● Police: ☎ 19
● Tourist Police: ☎ 024 384 601
● Fire/Ambulance: ☎ 15

MONEY

Moroccan dirhams (MAD or dh). Banknotes come in denominations of 20, 50, 100 and 200 dirhams. Coins come in denominations of 1, 2, 5 and 10 dirhams and 5, 10, 20 and 50 centimes.

10 dirhams

20 dirhams

100 dirhams

500 dirhams

ELECTRICITY

The local supply is 220 volts, 50Hz, using two-pin round plugs, as used in France. The old system of 110V is not very common in the hotels and riads you are likely to visit. Remember to bring a travel adaptor from home.

GRATUITIES/TIPS

Hotels (if service not included)	10 per cent
Restaurants (service not included)	10–15 per cent
Cafés/bars	10 per cent
Taxis	10 per cent
Massage/Spa Attendants	5 per cent
Doormen	change
Directions	change
Toilets	change

EMBASSIES AND CONSULATES

UK: ☎ 024 420 846
Germany: ☎ 037 653 605
USA: ☎ 022 267 151
Netherlands: ☎ 022 221 820
Spain: ☎ 037 687 470

HEALTH ADVICE

Sun advice Drink plenty of water and take regular breaks when walking. Treat dehydration symptoms (e.g. diarrhoea) as soon as possible.
Dentists and doctors If required, ask your hotel to recommend a reliable private dentist or *médecin généraliste* (GP).
Drugs Bring prescriptions for medicines you need. Pharmacies sell a wide range of drugs without controls. Be wary of their advice for all but minor ailments.

MONEY AND PRICES

Local currency (▷ panel this page) can't be exchanged at home, so bring your debit/credit card (▷ panel opposite) or travellers' cheques. The latter can involve queuing at banks and poor exchange rates. On departure, you can't spend dirhams beyond passport control or even on the national Moroccan airline.

Prices in Marrakech, and hotel rates, are comparable to prices in Europe and the US, as is dining out, especially if you drink wine, beer or spirits with your meal. As for souk souvenirs, similar items are competitively priced on the Internet, but of course it all depends on how good you are at haggling.

NATIONAL HOLIDAYS
Some of Morocco's national holidays are based on the Islamic Lunar Calendar. Dates for these events (asterisked) are given for the Western year of 2009, but will come around 11 days earlier each subsequent year.

1 Jan	New Year's Day
11 Jan	Manifesto of Independence
9 Mar	*Aïd al-Mawlid (Prophet's Birthday)
1 May	Labour Day
30 Jul	Feast of the Throne
14 Aug	Fête Oued Eddahab (Oued Eddahab Allegiance Day)
20 Aug	Révolution du Roi et du Peuple (The King and the People's Revolution Day)
14 Aug	Fête Oued Eddahab (Oued Eddahab Allegiance Day).
21 Aug	King Mohamed's Birthday
21 Sep	*Aïd al-Fitr (End of Ramadan—moveable).
6 Nov	Marche Verte (Anniversary of the Green March)
18 Nov	Fête de l'Indépendence (Independence Day)
28 Nov	*Aïd al-Adha (Feast of the Sacrifice—moveable)
18 Dec	*Fatih Muharram (Islamic New Year—moveable).

PERSONAL APPEARANCE AND BEHAVIOUR
Women who display bare arms, legs, neck or cleavage give offence and draw curious looks. A thin shawl covers your arms and chest, and will protect you from the sun and unwanted attention. Think twice before wearing high

PHOTOGRAPHS
● Locals, especially women, don't appreciate being photographed as curiosities.
● Always ask before taking a picture.
● In tourist hot-spots, you may be asked for money in return for a photo.
● Poverty is rife, and your small change might well feed a family.

PERSONAL SAFETY
● Crime is low here.
● The ubiquitous plain-clothed Tourist Police inflict harsh penalties on offenders.
● There is little hassle on the streets.
● Even pick-pocketing is not the problem it once was.

CREDIT CARDS
● ATMs are plentiful, dotted around Jemaa El Fna, and at most city banks.
● You may see begging at ATMs in the medina, but bear in mind that charity is considered a duty of Islam and begging here may not carry the stigma it does at home.
● Credit cards are widely accepted in hotels and upmarket shops, but in the souks cash is king for small purchases.
● For larger purchases, the seller might accept a card.

Essential Facts

OPENING HOURS

● Shops: 9–1, 3.30–7.30
Attractions/Museums:
Generally 8.30–6, sometimes
closing for lunch
Post Offices: 8–2, 3–6.30
Pharmacies: 9–1, 3.30–7.30
● Shops in the New City
close on Sundays. The souks
are closed Friday mornings,
stay open until 9pm or later,
and do not close for lunch or
on Sundays.

WHAT'S ON WHEN

Pick up the free monthly
entertainment guide,
Marrakech Pocket (www.
marrakechpocket.com) from
shops and hotels. Although
all in French, it's easy
enough to spot the latest art
exhibitions, cultural events,
bar openings etc. *Last Exit*
is a welcome addition to the
tourism magazine scene and
one of the few in English.
Glossy pages carry advertising for well-chosen opera-
tions and the articles are a
breath of fresh air. It is found
in hotels, restaurants and in
tourist offices.

heels to dinner in the medina, as uneven cobbles
are almost everywhere.

POSTAL SERVICES

The main PTT (post) office is in Guéliz at Place 16
Novembre, on the corner of Avenue Mohamed V
and Hassan II. (🕐 Mon–Sat 8am–2pm). There
is also a PTT on Jemaa El Fna (🕐 Mon–Thu
8.30–12, 2–6.30, Fri 8.30–11.30, 3–6.30,
Sat 8.30–11.30).

TELEPHONES

A GSM-900 mobile phone with roaming
activated will work in Morocco, but calls will be
exorbitant. For a long visit, bring an unlocked
phone from home and buy a pre-paid Moroccan
SIM card in town at Maroc Telecom or Méditel
outlets. For short visits, get a phonecard from
tobacconists or newspaper stands, for use in
public payphones. As always, dialling direct from
your hotel room incurs a hefty surcharge. For all
calls within Morocco, use the full area code. So,
include 024 (which has replaced 044) when
dialling a local Marrakech number. For restaurants and the like, get your hotel to call for you.
To dial a Marrakech number from abroad, the
international access code is +212, followed
by the city code without the 0, then the local
number.

INTERNATIONAL DIALLING CODES

From Morocco to:
UK: 00 44
Germany: 00 49
USA and Canada: 00 1
Netherlands: 00 31
Spain: 00 34

TIME DIFFERENCES

GMT	12 Noon
Marrakech	12 Noon
Germany	1pm
USA (NY)	7am
Netherlands	1pm
Spain	1pm

Moroccans speak their own version of Arabic and various dialects of Berber. In Marrakech, French is widely understood and many restaurant and hotel workers understand basic English.

USEFUL WORDS AND PHRASES

Do you speak English?	Itkelim Ingleezi
I don't understand	Mafhemsh
yes	eeyeh, naam
no	la
hello (to Muslims)	as Salaam alaykum
Response (to Muslims)	wa alaykum salaam
hello (informal)	La bes
response (informal)	bikheer
goodbye	bislemah
please	min fadlka (fadlik) / afek
thank you	shukran
God willing	Imshallah

NUMBERS

0	zifeer	7	sabbah
1	waahid	8	tamaniyah
1st	al'awwal	9	tissah
2	ith'nahn	10	asharah
2nd	athanee	20	eshreen
3	thalatha	100	mi'ah
3rd	athaleeth	200	mi'atahn
4	arbaa	500	khamseen
5	khamah	1000	alef
6	zeetta	2000	alfahn

IN THE MARKET

market	souk
it's expensive	Innahoo galee
How much is it?	Kam siaro hatha?
Another colour?	Lawanan axar?
Where is the mirror?	Aynal mir'ah?
enough	kafee
open	mahlul
closed	mahdud

GETTING AROUND

I'm lost	Ana T'left
Where is...?	Feyn...?
mosque	gaama; masjid
near / far?	kareeb / baeed
left / right	yassar / yemeen
straight on	neeshan
How many kilometres?	Kam kilomet?

HEALTH

pharmacy	farmasyan
clinic	chiyadah
doctor	tabeeb
medicine	dawa'a
pain	alam
diarrhoea	is'hal
dizziness	dawsah

FOOD FOR THOUGHT

restaurant	mataam
breakfast	iftar
lunch	yada'a
dinner	chasha'a
egg	beyd
bread	khobz
butter	zibda
coffee	kahwa
meat	leham
fish	samak
chicken	dajaj
I don't eat...	Makanakulsh...

Timeline

LORD OF THE ATLAS

Thami El Glaoui lived like the 'Lord of the Atlas' that he was during the first half of the 20th century. He entertained and seduced European beauties in his palace, torturing his enemies in the dungeons below and partied with international royalty and rulers. A despot warlord installed by the French imperialists as a puppet ruler, he turned the tables on them and united the Berber tribes in the north and south of the country, winning a degree of autonomy for his people.

1062 Berbers, the original inhabitants, build the fortified city of Marrakech (the Arab name for Morocco) during the great Almoravid Dynasty.

1147 The Almohad Dynasty destroys the beautiful city created by the Almoravids and build their own magnificent buildings, including the Koutoubia Mosque.

1269 Capital city moves to Fez after the Almohad Dynasty falls.

1554 Founding of the mighty Saâdian Dynasty, during which the spectacular Palais El Badii and the Tombeaux Saâdians, burial places of the great rulers of the Saâdian, are built.

1672–1727 Rule of cruel Moulay Ismail, known as the 'Warrior King', who imposes the Alaouite Dynasty and strips Palais El Badii bare.

1894 Moderniser Moulay Hassan—the last real Sultan of Morocco—dies and his ten-year-old son accedes to throne. This leads to European powers increasingly intervening in court matters.

1912 The French impose Imperial Rule, ratified by the Treaty of Fez.

1922 The Moroccan Rail Company builds the grand Mamounia Hotel.

From the left:
Gateway to the ramparts at Palais el Badii; King Mohamed VI; Koutoubia Mosque; tiled wall detail at the Tombeaux Saâdiens; Kasbah mosque and minaret, Tombeaux Saâdiens

1956 After years of inequality and poverty, the Moroccan people gain independence from France.

1961 King Hassan II succeeds his father Mohamed V.

1962 Morocco's first constitution is ratified in a referendum held in December.

1999 Accession to the throne of Mohamed VI. Although young and progressive, the king abuses his power.

2004 British man in Morocco jailed for homosexuality—a crime that carries a three-year sentence.

2005 Morocco's Equity and Reconciliation Commission recognizes past appalling human rights abuses.

2008 Morocco continues to repress women and those who speak out against the king, Islam or 'Moroccanness', and dissenting journalists are imprisoned. A Moroccan man is given a three-year jail sentence for masquerading as the king's brother on Facebook, but is later pardoned. The king's 'Vision 2010' plan for tourism is implemented.

2010 The year of fruition of King Mohamed VI's initiative to bring 10 million tourists to Morocco.

ALL ABOARD

In 1966, Crosby Stills and Nash wrote the happy, catchy *Marrakech Express* about the iconic train. This was the year that Brian Jones of the Rolling Stones first visited Morocco. Mick Jagger, John Lennon, Cecil Beaton and thousands of hippies followed in their footsteps, in a haze of drug-fuelled licentiousness that lasted through the 1970s—ironically, one of the most repressive decades for the Moroccan people.

NEED TO KNOW TIMELINE

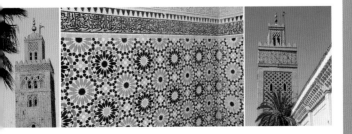

Index

CITYPACK TOP 25
Marrakech

WRITTEN BY Jane Egginton
BOOK DESIGN Keith Miller
EDITORIAL MANAGEMENT Apostrophe S Limited
INDEXER Marie Lorimer
SERIES EDITOR Marie-Claire Jefferies

© **AUTOMOBILE ASSOCIATION DEVELOPMENTS LIMITED 2009**

First published 2009

Colour separation by Keenes, Andover
Printed and bound by Leo Paper Products, China

A CIP catalogue record for this book is available from the British Library.

ISBN 978-0-7495-6023-2

All rights reserved. No part of this publication may be reproduced, stored in a retrieval system or transmitted in any form or by any means – electronic, photo-copying, recording or otherwise – unless the written permission of the publishers has been obtained beforehand. This book may not be lent, resold, hired out or otherwise disposed of by way of trade in any form of binding or cover other than that in which it is published, without the prior consent of the publishers.

The contents of this publication are believed correct at the time of printing. Nevertheless, the publishers cannot be held responsible for any errors or omissions or for changes in the details given in this guide or for the consequences of any reliance on the information provided by the same. This does not affect your statutory rights. Assessments of attractions, hotels, restaurants and so forth are based upon the author's own personal experience and, therefore, descriptions given in this guide necessarily contain an element of subjective opinion which may not reflect the publishers' opinion or dictate a reader's own experiences on another occasion. We have tried to ensure accuracy in this guide, but things do change and we would be grateful if readers would advise us of any inaccuracies they may encounter.

Published by AA Publishing, a trading name of Automobile Association Developments Limited, whose registered office is Fanum House, Basing View, Basingstoke, Hampshire RG21 4EA. Registered number 1878835.

A03606
Maps in this title produced from map data supplied by:
   Global Mapping, Brackley, UK (www.globalmapping.uk.com) Copyright
©Global Mapping/Kartographie Huber/The XYZ Digital Map Company
   Source: *Marrakech, Cartoville Gallimard* ©Gallimard Loisirs 2008

The Automobile Association would like to thank the following photographers, companies and picture libraries for their assistance in the preparation of this book.

Abbreviations for the picture credits are as follows; (t) top; (b) bottom; (l) left; (r) right; (c) centre; (AA) AA World Travel Library; (AM) Anna Mockford; (NB) Nick Bonetti.

1 AA/AM & NB; 2 AA/AM & NB; 3 AA/AM & NB; 4t AA/AM & NB; 4cl AA/AM & NB; 5t AA/AM & NB; 5b AA/AM & NB; 6t AA/AM & NB; 6cl AA/AM & NB; 6c AA/AM & NB; 6cr AA/AM & NB; 6bl AA/AM & NB; 6bc AA/AM & NB; 6br AA/AM & NB; 7t AA/AM & NB; 7cl AA/AM & NB; 7ccl AA/AM & NB; 7ccr AA/AM & NB; 7cr AA/AM & NB; 7bl AA/AM & NB; 7bcl AA/AM & NB; 7bcr AA/AM & NB; 7br AA/AM & NB; 8 AA/AM & NB; 9 AA/AM & NB; 10t AA/AM & NB; 10t AA/AM & NB; 10ctr AA/AM & NB; 10cr AA/AM & NB; 10cbr AA/AM & NB; 10/11 AA/AM & NB; 11t AA/AM & NB; 11ctl AA/AM & NB; 11cttl AA/AM & NB; 11cl AA/AM & NB; 11cbl AA/AM & NB; 12t AA/AM & NB; 12bl AA/AM & NB; 12br AA/AM & NB; 13t AA/AM & NB; 13ctl AA/AM & NB; 13cl AA/AM & NB; 13cbl AA/AM & NB; 13bl AA/AM & NB; 14t AA/AM & NB; 14ctl AA/AM & NB; 14cttl AA/AM & NB; 14cl AA/AM & NB; 14cbl AA/AM & NB; 14bl AA/AM & NB; 15t AA/AM & NB; 15b AA/AM & NB; 16t AA/AM & NB; 16ctr AA/AM & NB; 16cr AA/AM & NB; 16cbr AA/AM & NB; 16br AA/AM & NB; 17t AA/AM & NB; 17ctl AA/AM & NB; 17cl AA/AM & NB; 17cbl AA/AM & NB; 17bl Branx X Pics; 18t AA/AM & NB; 18ctr Brand X Pics; 18cr AA/AM & NB; 18ctr AA/AM & NB; 18br AA/AM & NB; 19t AA/AM & NB; 19ct AA/AM & NB; 19c AA/AM & NB; 19cb AA/AM & NB; 19b AA/AM & NB; 20/21 AA/AM & NB; 24t AA/AM & NB; 24cl AA/AM & NB; 24c AA/AM & NB; 24cr AA/AM & NB; 25tl AA/AM & NB; 25tr AA/AM & NB; 25cl AA/AM & NB; 25cr AA/AM & NB; 26l AA/AM & NB; 26r AA/AM & NB; 26/27 AA/AM & NB; 27t AA/AM & NB; 27c AA/AM & NB; 27cr AA/AM & NB; 28tl AA/AM & NB; 28tr AA/AM & NB; 28c AA/AM & NB; 29l AA/AM & NB; 29tr AA/AM & NB; 29cr AA/AM & NB; 30tl AA/AM & NB; 30r AA/AM & NB; 30cl AA/AM & NB; 31tl AA/AM & NB; 31tr AA/AM & NB; 31c AA/AM & NB; 32t AA/AM & NB; 32c AA/S McBride; 32b AA/AM & NB; 33t AA/AM & NB; 33bl AA/AM & NB; 33br AA/AM & NB; 34t AA/AM & NB; 34b AA/AM & NB; 35 AA/AM & NB; 36 AA/AM & NB; 37 AA/AM & NB; 38 AA/AM & NB; 39 AA/AM & NB; 40 AA/AM & NB; 41 AA/AM & NB; 44l AA/AM & NB; 44r AA/AM & NB; 45l AA/AM & NB; 45r AA/AM & NB; 46l Photolibrary Group; 46r Photolibrary Group; 47l AA/AM & NB; 47r AA/AM & NB; 48l AA/AM & NB; 48r AA/AM & NB; 49l AA/AM & NB; 49c AA/AM & NB; 49r AA/AM & NB; 50l AA/AM & NB; 50r AA/AM & NB; 50/51 AA/AM & NB; 51t AA/AM & NB; 51r AA/AM & NB; 52l AA/AM & NB; 52r AA/AM & NB; 52/53 AA/AM & NB; 53l AA/AM & NB; 53r AA/AM & NB; 54t AA/AM & NB; 54b AA/AM & NB; 55t AA/AM & NB; 55bl AA/AM & NB; 55br AA/AM & NB; 56 AA/AM & NB; 57 AA/AM & NB; 58 AA/AM & NB; 59 AA/AM & NB; 60 AA/AM & NB; 61 AA/AM & NB; 64l AA/AM & NB; 64c AA/AM & NB; 64r AA/AM & NB; 65l AA/AM & NB; 65r AA/AM & NB; 66 AA/AM & NB; 66/67t AA/AM & NB; 66/67b AA/AM & NB; 67t AA/AM & NB; 67c AA/AM & NB; 68l AA/AM & NB; 68c AA/AM & NB; 68r AA/AM & NB; 69 AA/AM & NB; 70t AA/AM & NB; 70cl AA/AM & NB; 70cr AA/AM & NB; 71l AA/AM & NB; 71tr AA/AM & NB; 71cr AA/AM & NB; 72t AA/AM & NB; 72bl AA/AM & NB; 72br AA/AM & NB; 73t AA/AM & NB; 73b AA/AM & NB; 74 AA/AM & NB; 75 AA/AM & NB; 76 AA/AM & NB; 77 AA/AM & NB; 80tl AA/AM & NB; 80tr AA/AM & NB; 80c AA/AM & NB; 81 AA/AM & NB; 82l AA/AM & NB; 82r AA/AM & NB; 82/83 AA/AM & NB; 83l AA/AM & NB; 83r AA/AM & NB; 84tl AA/AM & NB; 84tr AA/AM & NB; 84c AA/AM & NB; 85l AA/AM & NB; 85tr AA/AM & NB; 85cr AA/AM & NB; 86l AA/AM & NB; 86c AA/AM & NB; 86r AA/AM & NB; 87t AA/AM & NB; 87bl AA/AM & NB; 87br AA/AM & NB; 88t AA/AM & NB; 88cl AA/AM & NB; 88bl AA/AM & NB; 88br AA/AM & NB; 89 AA/AM & NB; 90 AA/AM & NB; 91 AA/AM & NB; 92 AA/AM & NB; 93 AA/AM & NB; 94/95 AA/AM & NB; 98 AA/AM & NB; 99tl AA/AM & NB; 99tr AA/AM & NB; 99cl AA/AM & NB; 99cr AA/AM & NB; 100t AA/AM & NB; 100cl AA/AM & NB; 100cr AA/AM & NB; 101tl AA/AM & NB; 101tr AA/AM & NB; 101c AA/AM & NB; 102l AA/AM & NB; 102r AA/AM & NB; 103t AA/AM & NB; 103cl AA/AM & NB; 103cr AA/AM & NB; 104l AA/AM & NB; 104r AA/AM & NB; 105t AA/I Burgum; 105bl AA/S McBride; 105br AA/S McBride; 106 AA/AM & NB; 107 AA/AM & NB; 108t AA/C Sawyer; 108ctl AA/AM & NB; 108cl AA/AM & NB; 108cbl AA/AM & NB; 108bl AA/AM & NB; 109 AA/C Sawyer; 110 AA/C Sawyer; 111 AA/C Sawyer; 112 AA/C Sawyer; 113 AA/AM & NB; 114 AA/AM & NB; 115 AA/AM & NB; 116 AA/AM & NB; 117t AA/AM & NB; 117b AA/AM & NB; 118t AA/AM & NB; 118b AA/AM & NB; 119t AA/AM & NB; 119c AA/AM & NB; 120 AA/AM & NB; 121 AA/AM & NB; 122 AA/AM & NB; 123 AA/AM & NB; 124t AA/AM & NB; 124bl AA/AM & NB; 124br AA/AM & NB; 125t AA/AM & NB; 125bl AA/AM & NB; 125bc AA/AM & NB; 125br AA/AM & NB

Every effort has been made to trace the copyright holders, and we apologise in advance for any accidental errors. We would be happy to apply the corrections in the following edition of this publication.